Marcus Harrison Green's incisive, big-hearted writing always stands out. He nails a high-difficulty landing every time, displaying the rare patience and empathy necessary to understand how someone can come to any point of view, while wielding the moral clarity and sociological insight that forces us to confront our own failures in facing the truth about poverty and racism. Along the way, he writes about himself with deep vulnerability in a way that illuminates not himself but the subjects of his writing, whom he clearly loves.

More writers should emulate the way Green makes humanity and hope burst forth from the dispiriting statistics we see everyday. He never stops at "Why is this happening?", instead persuading us to ask ourselves, "What are we doing about it?"

~Lawrence Lanahan, *The Lines Between Us*

Writing is a tool of exploration, and readers of Marcus' work get the benefit of his deep dives into family relationships, mental health, racial dynamics and many other parts of life that people leave largely unexamined because looking too closely feels perilous. Readers who go along with Marcus on his fearless journey in Readying to Rise *may be inspired to look more closely at themselves and the world.*

~Jerry Large, former *Seattle Times* columnist

In this invigorating collection of essays and speeches, celebrated orator and columnist Marcus Harrison Green calls readers to act upon the claims of our collective conscience. Readying to Rise *made me feel seen but not scolded. By combining personal stories with political insights, Green forges a path for those willing to engage with this world that so direly needs our efforts.*

~Kristen Millares Young, journalist, essayist & author of *Subduction*

Long before America's reckoning on racism and historical injustice, Marcus Harrison Green was busy peering into the nation's psyche—and examining his own. These incisive essays, some outward looking and others tenderly personal, show why his vision of journalism as a force for social good is so suited for our times. Marcus wears his heart on his sleeve, as everyone in his beloved South Seattle knows, but as a Black man in a nation that's only beginning to see the dignity of those who've been rendered powerless, he's under no illusions about the hard work that will be required for this country face its sins and at last, make us all feel at home.

These are of the chronicles of a nation wrestling with whether to reach for the best of itself, a man bearing his soul and a journalist coming to terms with his calling.

~Tyrone Beason, Journalist, *Los Angeles Times*

In a period in American History where so much we see and hear is false—Donald Trump was duly elected in 2020; patriots, tourists did not attack the Capitol on January 6th—Marcus Harrison Green's collection of essays is full of the truth. He understands that truth is not relative. Though some of the truth he explains, expounds may hurt, we may indeed be saved by these truths. One of his favorite quotations comes from Michel De Montaigne: The value of life lies not in the length of days, but in the use we make of them…Whether you find satisfaction in life depends not on your tale of years, but on your will. May he have many days because the world needs the truths he so clearly presents.

~Georgia McDade, Author *Outside the Cave*

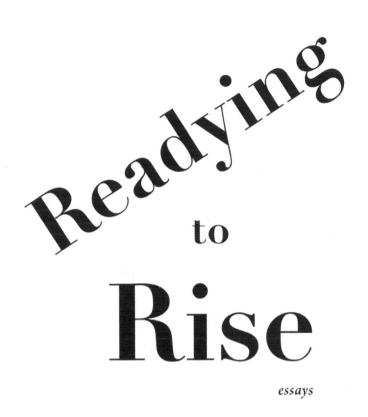

Readying

to

Rise

essays

by

MARCUS HARRISON GREEN

Foreword by Sonya Green Ayears

Continue to rise!!!
— Mr. Harrison Green

VERTVOLTA
PRESS

*Page 188 serves as information for the
original publications of all essays.*

Introduction © 2021 Sonya Green Ayears

Book design, cover & illustration: Vladimir Verano

*The publisher wishes to acknowledge
Erin K. Wilson for editorial assistance.*

print: 978-1-60944-143-2

e-book: 978-1-60944-144-9

Published in the United States by
VERTVOLTA PRESS
2614 CALIFORNIA AVE SW #236
SEATTLE, WA 98116

publisher@vertvoltapress.com

vertvoltapress.com

Please contact the publisher for Library of Congress Catalog Data

To my parents, Phillip and Cynthia

Contents

INTRODUCTION

BY

SONYA GREEN AYEARS

AFTER MARCUS DECIDED TO LEAVE A SUCCESSFUL, lucrative career in finance in Los Angeles, he returned to Seattle. This is where I met him, eager and ready to be a journalist. I was a news director at a public radio station in Seattle. Marcus sent me an email expressing his interest to be a volunteer reporter. I will admit, I was skeptical. If only I could count the amount of emails I received regularly from folks who confessed their love of radio and their desire to be on the air. The desire to be on the air being the key point. People wanted to be a radio reporter but rarely did they want to do the unglamorous job of reporting. This was not Marcus. He was earnest and very serious about wanting to do the work. I invited him to my office to meet.

From the start, I was rooting for Marcus. He was a published author of a novel, *A Year Without April*, when we met. It was clear his writing skills were superb. But it was more than his writing, it was his ambition to use the power of his pen to evoke change and make a difference in the world. Marcus knew he wanted to tell the stories of his home, his love, his muse: South Seattle. It was that singular mission and focus that has served him and the community he serves well.

Just Outside Utopia [the earlier title of this volume] is an apt metaphor for the life Marcus has lived thus far. He has long seen himself as an outsider, someone on the margins who can experience a sprinkle of goodness but never fully able to grasp it because of the many isms that linger in every corner, ready to steal his joy at any moment. Racism. Sexism. Ableism. Life has been bittersweet. Knowing this seems to make Marcus push even harder in pursuing truth and justice like it is oxygen.

Many people spout the words of Ralph Waldo Emerson, Life is a journey, not a destination. For most of those who say it, I often wonder if they fully embrace the meaning and live by the mantra. Marcus is one of the few people who I have met who embodies the message and lives life by those words.

When you read his impassioned essays, you can see why. Marcus has a vision for a world unseen but not unattainable. His power lies in his ability to manifest this vision through his words (and actions). He lays bare the problem and offers many solutions, chief among them: love. But do not mistake this love for an easy love. For to demonstrate this love truly means transformation.

I could not be more different than Marcus. I, a non-practicing, spiritual Christian who believes in God. Marcus, a non-practicing agnostic who does not believe in God. Yet, this is why our friendship or rather our kinship has endured. It is the ability to be different but still see and celebrate one another's humanity. It is this very simple act that Marcus is challenging us all to do daily and wholeheartedly.

Are you living life loudly? If not, ask yourself why. Marcus asks the question, "Will you live?" But the next question implied in his words is, "How will you live?"

Marcus challenges us all to be active participants, not passive-aggressive bystanders.

As I read *Readying to Rise*, James Baldwin's quote never left my head, "I love America more than any other country in the world and, exactly for this reason, I insist on the right to criticize her perpetually."

Marcus is a truth-teller. He explores topics of racism, equity, depression, mental illness, family and loss all with the precision of a surgeon that makes you cringe or flinch. He dissects his own role in patriarchy and reveals the ugly truths that we all have to face if social justice is really the goal. He provides a sober reminder of all of our privileges, earned and unearned.

The truth in the context of this book serves as the light. And the light, as a pastor once said to me, cleanses. Marcus might reject the notion of God but he invokes the very nature of his work through demanding more from us as humans.

The truth is in his self-reflection and honesty about his own attitudes toward racism and self-hatred. The truth is in his very personal battle with bipolar disorder and attempting suicide.

By the grace of God (yes, I am invoking God again) possibly working through his mother, Marcus is still with us today. I selfishly like to think he lived to share his powerful story which he lays bare, with raw emotions, bitter honesty and beautiful truth. His story is our story. An American story.

READYING TO RISE

The March Up the Mountaintop

When I was first asked to speak here today, I was tasked with answering whether or not society had reached Martin Luther King's "mountaintop of racial harmony," I'll have to be honest. My initial thought was, how the hell does anyone expect this speech to surpass three seconds.

But after realizing I was, in fact, expected to deliver more than one syllable, the question prompted deeper reflection. It actually took me back to a day seven years ago, the last day of my grandfather's life.

It proved an enchanted day for the both of us.

January 20, 2009. I remember it vividly. To me that day was the height of what it meant to be Black in this country, the day I thought we'd reached that mountaintop—that was certainly the mood at the time. It was the day an African-American man finally strolled with his family down Washington's Pennsylvania Avenue to get sworn into the highest office in this nation.

Cloud nine wasn't high enough for me that day—I was on cloud infinity to the fifth power, and what made it sweeter, what made it even more memorable, was that I shared it with my grandfather. He had been debilitated by a heart condition for months, but on that day he got up the strength to watch the inauguration.

My grandfather, Jimmie Green, was not an emotional man. Growing up, I never once believed he was capable of shedding a tear. But that day he couldn't help but be overcome with joy, the type of joy that only comes when you finally see something that for so long you've been told is impossible.

And so I asked him—I asked this man who had grown up a sharecropper in a segregated Arkansas; who, because of the laws at that time, was forbidden from going beyond an eighth-grade education; who had been called "boy" so long it took him until his late twenties to fully believe he was a man; who wasn't allowed to fight for this country in a segregated military, but was allowed to cook for the soldiers who did; and who couldn't cast a vote for a president until he was 35—I asked my grandfather if he ever thought a man who looked like the one he voted for that November could ever become president.

"No," he answered. "No, I never, ever dreamed a day like this was possible."

"But, Marcus," he cautioned, "be careful, because as good of a day as this is, it's just one, and we need many more. We still have higher to rise."

That's the last thing he ever told me. Later that night he fell into a coma and passed away, having seen the impossible.

But his words always stuck with me, though they were hard to process at first.

It was difficult to not be seduced by the notion that our society had finally vanquished its race problem. That we had now ushered in a golden era of "colorblindness."

It's hard, almost impossible, for us to not be seduced by the pervasive assumption that we are more than 90 percent of the way to racial utopia. Somehow we are supposed to believe that this nation's history—one of genocide, slavery, suppression, and exclusion—cannot possibly impact its present or future. That blatant acts of racism are now few and far between, relegated to the margins of simple-minded militia members in western Oregon or the bloviating, fascist presidential candidates they lovingly support.

We can point to the room that has been made for people of color and women at the top of our society's totem pole, their high visibility in positions of power.

We can point out that explicit forms of racism have been on the wane since MLK spoke of his mountaintop. No more are there police dogs that ravage the bodies of marchers; no more are there billy clubs that fracture the skulls of protesters, or water hoses to impede their progress. No more are there signs to designate where we can or cannot be seated or served.

I hear that racism is dead from some of my own black brothers when discussing the case of Sandra Bland, the woman mysteriously found dead in her prison cell after a routine traffic stop, or the case of John Foster, killed within seconds of Ohio police arriving to a Wal-Mart for holding a BB gun.

Many of them—long conditioned to what they call "proper" interaction with law enforcement—tell me that Bland and Foster should have known to mind their behavior in front of an officer, that ultimately the two are responsible for their own deaths.

I hear tales of racism's demise so often from my liberal white brothers and sisters, who spout that the true culprit is a crisis of culture, a lack of personal responsibility, and a chronic condition of moral malaise.

I hear of its end in the midst of a society whose black infants are three times more likely than white infants to die within the first months of birth, despite no biological deficiency.

I hear racism is a relic in a society that mocks the provision of safe spaces for its marginalized students while actively creating safety for those it values.

I read racism's obituary even after a recent reporting trip, when a white mother told me that she could never know what it was like to suffer in the same way that a black mother does in this country, because if her 12-year-old child were to be killed by a police officer, her son's murder would be a crime.

No, racism is not dead. What it is now is sophisticated. What it is now is systemic.

It is like the Greek hydra, that beast that regenerates in a new form just as you've begun to celebrate its defeat.

For every Bettie Jones, needlessly killed by Chicago police responding to a dispute she had nothing to do with, it creates a million Yvettes who will die early deaths because they are economically bound to an area with limited access to healthcare.

For every Trayvon Martin, there will be a million Andres swallowed whole by a criminal justice system that will never offer a chance for redemption, that will forever brand them with a scarlet F for felon. Their lives, now absent of opportunity, will be nothing more than slow deaths.

As it was once housed prominently in the hearts of unrepentant bigots, racism stubbornly finds shelter in the institutions of our society and its systems.

The gears of these systems continue to be greased with black bodies, and function regardless of the good intentions of the men and women pulling the lever. It does not matter whether the hands of the people holding that lever are black, as they are in the city of Baltimore, or if those hands are white, as they are in Ferguson, Missouri.

Nor does it matter if they are brown, or beige, or metallic marble. The outcome is always the same: mass devastation of black life.

So, are we there yet? To ask the question in this country is to answer it.

But the racism we encounter today can't be solved by a civil rights-era understanding of what we face. In truth, we can't even entertain the question of "Are we there yet?" before answering a more important one: "Where are we now?"

That question is tougher, because we occupy different planes of existence in this country, and so we must be honest about our social locations. Because you can only know what direction to go by knowing exactly where you stand.

What guides us to our desired destination is a word that is so misused and cheapened by that misuse.

Love.

When I say the word, I say it as one that equates to the resiliency needed by those who fight for racial justice, to seemingly no avail, to the point that their knuckles are raw and bleeding, and yet they must continue to fight.

I say that word as synonymous with the acceptance necessary by those with bestowed advantages, whether because of pigment or class. Who must see past fragility and privilege and realize that to consider your life in context is not a demonstration of weakness, but an exhibition of character.

When all groups who have been discriminated against in this country sit down to eat at America's dinner table, it's love that asks the privileged to understand that when they see a race that has been malnourished for so long pleading to feed on America's promises, that race is not insisting that all others should starve—they are just trying to eat like everyone else.

I say love in a way that translates to faith—the faith required of all of us. Faith in what so often goes unseen in our human brethren. Faith in their capacity to change, their capacity to grow.

That word, and the deeds it inspires, is the only way I know to change this world. This world we live in by choice, and, yes, our collective circumstance is a choice.

We can live in the world we were born into, or we can live in the world as it can be.

I know that last point causes cynics to grind their teeth. They think this world we live in is the best of all possible worlds, that our present is as good as it can possibly be. But this world in its present state is constructed by no laws of nature. It is built on a foundation of the ideas, beliefs, and doctrines of people, and kept in place by fear, apathy, and resignation.

And it can only be undone by the new ideas, imagination, and beliefs of other people.

We can live in a society that puts a higher value on some lives, or we can choose to live in a society where all lives truly matter, including black ones, but we cannot have both.

We can live in the world we were born into, or we can live in the world as it can be.

This "world as it can be" isn't one left to fantasy, or one that only exists in dreams, no matter how noble. It is one being birthed right here, right now.

It is being birthed in the city of Seattle by Devan Rogers, a Seattle Central College student. She's a young woman who couldn't tolerate that, in this liberal bastion she calls home, more than half of all incarcerated juveniles are children of color, so she helped get that same city to pass a resolution to move toward the goal of zero-percent youth incarceration and an alternative to imprisonment.

It's birthed right here in this county named after Martin Luther King, Jr. by Bridgette Hempstead, who couldn't sit back any longer and abide the continuous health disparities found in unincorporated King County's Skyway area. Because of her effort, its mostly poor black and white population will soon have access to the health services long denied them.

It is birthed right here in the state of Washington by Dominique Davis, who was sick and tired of burying black, brown, red, and poor white youth, and is working to install violence prevention and racial sensitivity training in every school district in this state.

Respectively, they are a student, a semi-retired mother of three, and a part-time football coach. These people hold no elected office and they more than likely will never have a national holiday in their name.

They are people who possess nothing more than empathy, courage, resolve, and conviction.

They are people who embody Dr. King's legacy, a man who in all his reverence, in all his glory, was still just a man. A man who was as flawed and as human as we all are today.

Sainthood is not a requirement for progress.

I say that not to injure his legacy, but to truly do it justice. Because that legacy tells me that it doesn't matter one iota if you are fractured, broken, or bruised, because your participation in this world is mandatory to transform it.

His legacy tells me it doesn't matter whether your position is President of the United States or a Starbucks barista between dream jobs. Whatever your occupation, when you fight against hatred, you propel justice.

His legacy tells me that no matter how dark our days, there will be light. There will be hope. There is hope today, because we all woke up this morning. You woke up this morning with courage, conviction, and empathy at your disposal, the raw ingredients to heal this sick world, if you just choose to activate them.

That legacy tells me that there is no measure too small in our ascent up to Dr. King's mountaintop. So in a climb that no one person, no one generation, will complete alone, his legacy tells me it doesn't matter whether the actions you take to combat racial madness are measured in centimeters, inches, or feet. For our society, there are no insignificant steps upward.

Dr. King knew this when he told us in his last speech that he wouldn't get there with us. My grandfather knew this when he told me we still had far to go. I'll know this someday long from now, when my granddaughter asks me, "Grandfather, are we there yet?" and I'll tell her then the same exact thing that I'll tell you now.

I'll say to her we've climbed far, but we have farther still to rise, so now go reach up and pull us higher. You rise up and you pull us higher.

Superman Taught Me Most of What I Know About Life

I HAVE TO CONFESS IT'S A LITTLE EMBARRASSING to stand up here and admit as a 30-year-old man my unconditional affection for a comic book hero who wears red and blue pajamas. It's a love that I can trace back to when I was four years old and my mind attached itself to the basic idea of Superman—that yes, indeed, one person could make a difference. It seems like only yesterday that I snatched away my mother's red tablecloth and draped it around my shoulders as if it were a cape, taking off like a rocket down the street while she screamed frantically behind me in hot pursuit, yelling for me to come put it back before it got dirty, while all our neighbors laughed at our display. But no, that wasn't yesterday, that was actually last Tuesday. I guess that shows you how far I've evolved in 26 years.

There is a day, however, that actually does stand out profoundly as a day in my life that I wish I had been Superman.

I was living and working in Los Angeles at the time, and like a good son, I'd phone my mother who still lived in Seattle for our weekly Wednesday morning call, just to check in with her to see how everything was going back home. It ended up being one I could have missed. You see, my mother slogs through the daily grind of social work, so there are many days when she hears the worst of the worst, and many times it challenges her ability just to stay sane, as she often puts it to me, but this particular day took the cake. As we began our conversation I could tell by the breaking of her voice and her long pauses between thoughts that something ominous was brewing.

Unfortunately, my assumption proved correct. Her Tuesday had concluded with the death of Alajuwan Brown, a young boy from our neighborhood, just shy of his 13th birthday, who was nothing less than a delight to everyone he came across. He had been shot while coming home from purchasing a pair of football cleats he had spent the last three months saving up for by doing odd jobs around the community. He was killed for no other reason than that he happened to have gotten off the wrong bus, at the wrong time, wearing the wrong color, and was mistaken for a rival gang member by his shooter. To make matters worse, not two hours before that tragic shooting, my mother had received calls from a woman who had again been violently raped by her husband, right in front of their three children. He told her afterward that he would kill her and their kids if she tried to leave him or told anyone about what had transpired. This was a man who in our community was considered an upstanding person—"a good man of God ," as he was fond of calling himself. She wanted so desperately to get away from him, but for whatever reason, no shelter would take her and the children, and she had no other family besides her attacker to support her. This happened all in the same day—a day that had begun for my mother with a 14- year-old girl crying hysterically on the phone, barely able to catch her breath, as she shared that she was pregnant by her father, and had absolutely no idea what to do.

I would later christen that day a cure-all for the desire to live, as it would haunt me for quite some time. While driving to work I remember wishing, just wishing, that I could do something, that I could be a Superman who could turn back time and make all that was wrong, right. When I finally got to work, I related to a colleague of mine all that had taken place back in my hometown, and I recall exactly what he said to me. He said, "Marcus, that's just the world we live in, and if it isn't busy going to hell it's already there. You're not Superman, so really, what can you do besides grin and bear it? I mean, you can't change it, and really, who are you anyway to try?"

I had to admit that he was right—not about the trajectory of the world, at least not entirely—but he had been right to ask me, frankly, who was I to change it? That became a question that poured over every thought I had that day. Reason being, I didn't know. You see, in life we seem to be bombarded, whether at work or at play, whether by the cynicism of ourselves or others, with reminders of what we aren't. We aren't endowed with greatness, we aren't geniuses, we aren't influential, we aren't powerful, ergo, when it comes to the business of shaping this world, we are ultimately nothing more than children who should leave the activity of such things to the "adults" in the room or the elites at the table. The best we can possibly hope for is to go about our lives as regular people shopping, eating, surviving, and finding something to do to amuse ourselves in the time we're not occupied with the other three, repeating the cycle until death. We might as well find refuge in the sanctuary of selfish endeavors, building our own structure of solitude, while making an attempt to ignore all else around us as it crumbles.

On that day I could no longer accept that idea, and, like most non-practicing agnostics do when they're going through a crisis of conscience, I turned to Superman. However, it wasn't the one who flies in our fantasies, but the one who was unable to walk in real life. It just so happened that that night, an old interview with the late Christopher Reeve was on television. This was a man who had played the character of Superman in four feature films and is the actor most beloved for doing so, mainly because after being paralyzed in a tragic horse riding accident, he went on to embody what the word "hero" meant. In this particular interview, he explained its meaning.

He said, "A hero is no Superman, no angel, but an ordinary person, who in daring to act courageously without regard to any personal consequences, tests the limits of what others think we as human beings are capable of. They are the people who make changes others once thought were impossible in this world, inevitable."

It honestly took a while for that to sink in for me—the idea that neither strength nor sainthood was a requirement to be more than a bystander to the proceedings of this world. Because it was, after all, a serial adulterer who dreamt that the content of our character matters more than the color that covers our skin. It was, after all, a man who gave praise to Hitler and the theory of a superior, pure race, who imagined a world where peace reigned in every corner of it. And it was, after all, a woman who refused to speak out against the vile and inhumane practice of lynching who fought with unmatched fervor for the right of all women to be treated as justly as any man.

Now, I suppose that's a harsh and peculiar way to identify Martin Luther King, Jr., Gandhi, and Susan B. Anthony, and I don't mention their deficiencies for the sake of irreverence nor to diminish their achievements. On the contrary, I mention them to accentuate the fact that all great men and women are just that, men and women, human beings with flaws and failings that are not just exclusive to us mere mortals.

Instead of being disheartened by that revelation, it's that knowledge that comforts me; if what constitutes the worst of our heroes is not restricted from us, then neither is what constitutes the best of them. Their voices that spoke loudly for all those who couldn't find their own—well, we happen to come equipped with one. Their hearts that they bound to the progression of the condition of their brethren—well, one happens to beat in our chest cavity also. Their hands that authored the present we find ourselves in today, one free from the horrors of slavery, the absurdity of women's second class status, and the insanity of criminalizing the act of love between two people who happen to share the same gender—if you look down past your wrists, most of us will discover a pair of our own.

A voice, a heart, hands, and so many other things we find in ourselves that are so unremarkable: they serve as the same raw material that we share with all those idols we so admire. It is this material, which we all possess, that functions as a recourse for changing this world we find ourselves in.

Because we live in a world that is not fair and is not just. We live in a world with egregious inequity between the privileged few and the growing legion of the weak. We live in a world where we divide ourselves by the artificial distinctions of race and religion and sexuality. We live in a world that is far from perfect and most likely never will be. But fortunately, we also live in a world that comes with no default setting to it. There is no law of nature that decrees that things must always be how they are.

It is this world that we must face, one where there is no Superman to wait for. We often find that we are all we have, but what we also often find is that we are all we need, because this world cannot be saved by a Man of Steel, but by men and women of courage, of conviction, of empathy and of compassion. It can be saved by men and women who aren't invulnerable and who indeed feel pain, adversity, and failure—those additional ingredients that are so necessary to developing the ability to endure, overcome, and persevere on this earth we all share. Those abilities do more to shape this world than anything a superhuman can lay claim to.

I say that, not as a naive Pollyanna who has visions of utopia, but as a man who has glimpsed reality. I saw this in Alajuwan Brown's mother who now devotes her life, via her nonprofit, to mentoring and nurturing young boys and girls in our community, doing all she can to make sure that no more mothers must bury their sons. I saw this in the community of women who unequivocally supported the woman who had been raped by her sociopathic husband, providing asylum for her and her children from a life that was hell. I saw this in the uncle of the girl who had been impregnated by her father when he and his husband became the caregivers of her and her child, restoring her faith in the sacredness of family.

As admirable as these acts are, I have no delusions that they alone are enough to alter the course of our world. No one action, no one person can. What they function as, just like any act that encroaches upon all the darkness that surrounds us, is sparks. A reminder that this world, no matter how dim it may seem to us, contains illuminating possibilities. These acts that we pursue as individuals, when taken together, feed the flame that dares to oppose all that is evil around us.

It is at this point when we discover that we actually share a great deal with the fictional Superman. Like him, we sense that we live in a place that is so desperately in need of saving, and like him we encounter a decision of great importance. We can pretend to be as meek and as mild as Clark Kent when he puts on his glasses—going on about our lives, masking our true selves, hiding amongst the anonymity, afraid to stand out as we acquiesce to our imagined weaknesses—or we can take a hard look at ourselves, as I'm sure we often do, knowing that there is more inside of us than what we allow the world to see, more that we can accomplish than what others expect of us. And in recognizing this we can stand tall and remove our glasses, revealing to the world who we are—who we truly are—along with what we are truly capable of.

So, who are you? Who are you, really, to do anything in this world? The answer is simple, as it is the same for all of us. We are who we choose to be. No matter your choice, our world, our country, our state, our community, our neighbors, our friends, and our families, await your answer with great anticipation.

It Took Me Years to Believe That Black Lives Matter, Let Alone My Own

I ALWAYS BRAG TO MY FRIENDS THAT Westside Unitarian has the largest black congregation of any Unitarian Church in Washington State. And when I told one of my friends I was nervous about giving a sermon on racism here, he asked me just how large it actually was.

Five, I told him.

"Five percent," he said. "That's not bad for Washington!"

"No," I said. "Five people."

He said, "Marcus, I know you claim to be agnostic, so you're kind of on the fence on whether God exists on not. But if I were you I'd get down on my knees in some intense prayer to him to plead you're not lynched."

It wasn't just that one friend. Tons of people told me to stay away from the subject of race altogether. People said I was bound to offend someone, and that I'd anger more people than I'd inspire. And yes, they said, black lives matter. But so do white lives, and Asian lives, and Native American lives. All lives matter, they said.

I understand the reluctance to discuss race in this country. The topic challenges the fundamentals of our

American narrative, and threatens to undermine its dictum of personal fortunes determined exclusively by hard work, grit, and perseverance. In this narrative, the role of pigment is absent or insignificant.

For most, it is better not to speak of race, nor assess its prominence in our society. As Socrates knew, it is easier to live in a world that goes unexamined. Typically, that is a necessity in order for a society to tolerate reprehensible treatment of its members.

I do not stand here in judgment of that mindset today. I stand here as someone who once held it.

I used to believe, or wanted to believe, that racism was nothing more than the personal prejudices of the ignorant, who did not get the memo that the 21st century had arrived. I used to think our society had bigger fish to fry. That's how I learned to navigate being black in this country.

In first grade, I remember being told it was OK that I was stupid, because God didn't intend to make "people like me" as smart as my other classmates (all of them white). When I was 13 years old, a police officer stopped me as I crossed the street near my home for the heinous crime of jaywalking, so he could press my face into the hood of his car and whisper in my ear: "Nigger, I'll rape your mother and there's nothing you can do about it."

While in prep school, I was the only one to ever face punishment after fights with my white schoolmates. (I never started these fights, but for the record I won most of them.) When I made a six-figure salary working at a hedge fund in Los Angeles, I was told I was "one of the decent ones."

"Marcus," my manager told me, "Don't ever think we'll try to bring more of you in here. We don't want to be confused with Harlem."

For me, it was easier to live in denial. I latched onto the grand American gospel that says every ill you face can be traced back to personal responsibility. I told myself that if I acted more politely, didn't have a chip on my shoulder, and adapted well to different circumstances, I'd be fine. I felt the need to act more passive and less threatening.

I repeated this mantra so often that it became my truth. And that imprisoned me. It shackled me with self-hatred, and I began to extend those feelings toward my own race.

Every time a black person was shot down on the street, I shamelessly joined in the chorus: "If only they had pulled up their saggy pants." When a black person spoke out about injustice, my rapid-fire response was to apologize on behalf of black America.

I distanced myself from anything that was controversial. I found myself in a constant waltz on eggshells. I measured and weighed everything I saw and did not in relation to who I was, but to who I hoped white people saw me as.

My own thoughts, feelings, and dissatisfaction with this world no longer mattered.

I had so deeply internalized my own inferiority that it took a white person to rattle me back into reality.

I'd just begun my career as a reporter. She was a contact for a story I was working on. She called herself an antiracist organizer, which I thought was a code word for white-guilt cheerleader. She was organizing against the disproportionate numbers of black and brown youth incarcerated in King County's juvenile justice system, which includes the city of Seattle. Black and brown people made up a little less than 12 percent of the youth population, but 60 percent of the population in detention.

She explained that this pattern was common, and that this was a piece of a larger system that had long ago replaced explicit racism in America. It was a system that harbored racial biases in its policies and practices. It did not require racist people to achieve racist outcomes.

She broke down a system that allows black infant babies to die at twice the rate of white ones. A system that expels black kids from school at five times the rate of white kids. A system where black teenagers are more likely to die than graduate from college. A system where police kill black people 21 times more often than white people. And a system that cages more black men today than were in bondage during slavery.

It didn't take long after that discussion for me to dislodge myself from the illusions I'd harbored. The illusions that had kept me safe in this society kept me from being seen as just another angry black man.

But the thing is, I *am* angry. And I do not apologize for that.

My question is, why aren't you? Why are you willing to accept the lie that all lives matter in this country? All lives do not matter in this country, and rarely have they ever. And it is absurd to state otherwise.

And I know that some believe that to spotlight the plight of one race is to dismiss those of another.

But I hope you would not think that speaking of the Holocaust would somehow reduce the impact of the genocide done to Native Americans. Or that to speak of the persecution and mass bombings of Muslim mosques belittles the shootings and hate crimes at Jewish synagogues. I hope you would not think to mention the plight of migrant workers in America diminishes those of migrants from Syria traveling for their survival to Europe. I hope you can appreciate the uniqueness of these crises, rather than dissolving them into one another.

To say "Black Lives Matter" does not promote superiority. It gives a voice to people who continue to struggle to be heard and seen in this country. That is why we must shout, we must interrupt, and we must inconvenience, so it can say that I am here too, and I am dying, but I am trying so desperately hard to live.

To group these problems together with all others is to be as foolish, and as delirious, as to deny medical attention to a stuttering heart because your kidneys and lungs also ail.

To continually deny someone's humanity, someone's suffering, is to eventually deny your own humanity, and to invite suffering on yourself.

I've heard the things that often trail that statement. "I did not own slaves." "I did not kill anyone." "I have never been prejudiced against anyone, and therefore I should not be made to feel guilty."

And that may be true. You did not own slaves. You did not pull a trigger.

You are not responsible for being born into a country that exterminated Native Americans for land, enslaved Africans for work, exploited Asians, Mexicans, and Irish for labor, treated women as second-class citizens, and outlawed marriage for homosexuals.

No, it is not your fault that you have come into this world as it is. But it is your fault if you leave it that way when you go.

What you are responsible for is the same exact thing that everyone is responsible for, and that is the world as it *can* exist.

It is our fault if we allow black lives to be disproportionately punished, pillaged, and destroyed. It is our fault if we continue to live in a world that offers life rafts to some while leaving others to drown. It is our fault if we refuse to extend our consciousness beyond our own individual lives. It is our fault if we keep this system intact.

I know that there is pain in acknowledging racism. I know it requires good intentions be balanced with patience and deference. I know it requires silence at times in letting others speak. I know it requires self-examination that can take you to places you never wished to go. I know it requires the fortitude to be willing to be offended, to be called out, to feel uneasy—and to seek understanding through that uneasiness.

I know that's a lot to ask. But I've discovered that's how you articulate love in the clearest way possible.

I am looking forward to the day when that very thing is articulated by our hearts, our actions, and our institutions. When that day comes in this country, there will be no need to ever utter the words "Black Lives Matter" again.

Filling Your Own Cup

As someone whose profession demands that I traffic in reality, I can tell you that too often our society is repulsed by the very notion of truth.

It's more convenient to believe in a world that's inherently fair and just, than it is to confront one where patriarchy and racism might lose a round or two, but ultimately stand undefeated.

It's easier to believe in a life where everything you've received has solely been the product of your own labor, rather than just one of a multitude of variables such as luck and privilege.

It's easier to believe that you are who others advertise you to be, as opposed to who you are when there is no one watching. It's so much easier to prefer smoke over flame.

Delusion is the most powerful intoxicant in the world—and it has no more powerful variant than self-delusion.

I found this out myself the way most people learn: The hard way.

It was on a day not so far in the past, when I had hit my darkest point in life. Ironically, this was at a moment when, career-wise, I couldn't have flown higher.

I had accolades, awards, and acclaim for my writing. I had a sterling reputation to people outside my tight-knit circle, and a photogenic smile that defrosted the most stoic curmudgeons. I was called a future leader, destined for big things.

But beneath the surface was a hollowness. Beneath, there was a numbness that no amount of social justice treatises I wrote, speeches I gave, or stories I covered could fill.

And so I attempted to fill that with anything that made me feel alive ... or made me feel anything at all.

An over-reliance on alcohol and other people to provide me with wholeness soon turned into a dependence on them.

And that dependency gradually led to a series of days when I hurt someone I love. Thankfully, the hurt wasn't physical, but the pain from a betrayal of trust and of constant emotional exploitation can wound deeply.

Emotionally exhausted, she finally asked that I never speak to her again.

This wasn't the first time this kind of thing had happened. Yet again, I had hurt someone I cared for. Yet again, I'd tried to explain away my own behavior and actions as problems with the other person.

But something was different this time. After so many years of repeating the pattern, I couldn't so easily dismiss it. I couldn't sit with myself without shaking to the core with pain. In fact, I couldn't sit with myself at all. I was terrified of any invitation for introspection.

Instead, I engaged in self-hatred: I'm always going to be destined to repeat this; I'm always going to hurt the people I care about most. My closest relationships will always unravel.

For years I had battled deep depression, and for years, I had not accepted my diagnosis of bipolar disorder. For years, I thought the best treatment for the challenges I knew but didn't want to believe I had was to self-medicate with alcohol and the grace other people loaned me.

Neither was working anymore, though. And there was only one way out of this nightmare.

My mother will tell you that it was God who told her to come back to the house that day. I'm still not quite sure if he exists or not, but if he does, it had to be him who gave her the speed to run up and cut the power cord I had attached to my neck.

At the hospital she cupped my hand in hers for what seemed like forever, before she finally said: "I love you with all my heart. I love you unconditionally with all your flaws and all your pain, but I can't love you as much as you can love yourself. No one can.

"Can you love yourself?" she asked.

My response: "I don't know. I've never tried before."

You see, I had become conditioned by life to derive my value and worth vicariously through external mediums.

It's an easy trap to fall into when you've survived both a rich, predominantly white educational institution and a profession where you'll never be white enough or rich enough to fully be accepted. So you learn early on to don a personality that will place you as proximate as possible to those things.

It's easy to be snared into that mindset when you grow up in a poor area of the city, and because of your different social experience—the private schools you go to and music you listen to—you're never considered black enough. So every day, when the school bus drops you a mile away from your home, you have to fight, because another teen thinks you are better than them.

As you grow tired of fighting, you code switch your language, replicate troublesome behavior, and do whatever it takes to be fully absorbed into the crowd.

Different circumstances, but always the same message: You as you are not deserving of acceptance. You as you are are not deserving of love. To deserve those things, you must be anything other than what you are in your rawest and most honest form.

The habit of seeking outside validation and value proves a heavy chain to break as you get older.

You learn how simple it is to adapt to your surroundings, to repeal any didactic discomfort, to disengage from any challenges to your sacred self-image that has been crafted by the consensus of external actors.

To do anything else would spark an internal civil war, an inner mutiny too painful to undertake.

And so what you do becomes who you are. Your status becomes who you are. Your accomplishments become who you are. Your operatic "wokeness" becomes who you are. Your profession becomes who you are.

So much so that we would be lost, and forget who we are, without those flimsy tags marking us.

My badge read: "Person who wants to make the world a better place." I was someone who saw all the suffering, all the pain, all the oppression, all the hopelessness, and wanted to swoop in and elevate as much of it as I could.

I still believe wholeheartedly in the nobleness of those goals and continue to dedicate a good chunk of my life to that work.

But you see, in my rush to save the burning building called this world, I didn't recognize until it was almost too late that I myself was on fire.

I had compassion, kindness, and magnanimity, but had none left for myself. I allowed myself to be pulled in a thousand different directions, always coming to others' rescue while endangering myself.

I remember one day I was surrounded by hundreds of people celebrating the accomplishments of a publication I had started. They greeted me with praise on their tongues and joy in their hearts. Yet I had never felt so lonely in my life. I couldn't stand myself. I hated myself. Better to escape him through heavy drinking then spend any time with him.

But after the experience with my mother, heaven sent as she was or not, I realized I needed the kind of rendezvous with myself that I had been dreading for a decade.

Sitting with myself, alone, far away from everyone else, was terrifying. It was a time of thorough, comprehensive self-examination. It was a one-on-one with reality—and I didn't always like what reality told me. You see, reality owes us no comfort, no pleasure, and no satisfaction. I think that's why so many of us so rarely choose to deal with it, to apply a microscope to ourselves.

But the thing about being terrified and afraid is that it's an opportunity to cultivate courage and strength. The only time we can be courageous is when we are scared. The only time we can demonstrate strength is when we face weakness.

That was how I learned to accept myself—to no longer be at war with who I was.

Being bipolar means that every day is an adventure lived intentionally and deliberately. It's hard to be captive to a mind that regularly betrays you; it's hard when your actions at the most inopportune moments feel authored by another person. You ultimately have to surrender to the fact that you can't willpower your way out of it. You have to do the arduous work of managing it.

When you're sad, you pour tears. When you're angry, you combust, and when you're happy, you glow.

It takes a special person to love me. But after 36 years, I've finally found someone willing to try.

I wake up inside of him every day.

And the love he gives is clearly defined. The love he gives is not harmless; no, it is threatening, because the love he gives crumbles away all the untruth. It sees through all the facades, pretenses, and artifices I've constructed to get along through life.

The love he gives knows that I will never be perfect, but I am seeking improvement. It knows that I will never please everyone, but I can still impact some. It knows that my knowledge of the lived experiences of others different from me will never be fully complete, but I will make up the gap in my education.

It holds me accountable to live life as the best possible version of myself, armed with humility, grace, thoughtfulness, and most of all, an immense reverence for honest self-assessment.

It tells me that with all my flaws, with all my pain, with all my broken vows, with all my mistakes, abnormalities, and multitude of sins, I am worthy of love.

It took me so, so long to believe that and to know that—for that to become my reality. But I am so glad it is, because when that's your reality, you learn to face the day and this world so much differently. You learn to meet it not where it's at, but where you're at: In a state of loving transformation.

It's love that saved me, that changed me, that propels me this day. Where I was tiny, it's made me feel huge.

We cannot change this world without changing and loving ourselves first. As bad as things may be, this world can wait just a little while longer for you to save yourself.

May you find love within yourself.

What We Dread to Address

A CURE FOR THE WILL TO LIVE IS WHAT greeted me on the streets of South Seattle Monday night. The mood was like Vatican City moments following the pope's death. It was barely an hour after a different announcement—one made by a St. Louis grand jury. They had decided against indicting Ferguson, Missouri police officer Darren Wilson in the killing of Mike Brown, effectively absolving Wilson of any wrongdoing for fatally shooting the unarmed teenager on August 9th.

Stepping onto the light rail from Rainier Beach, I was met by faces that ran a narrow spectrum between anguish and disillusionment. There was the middle-aged black mother with tears silently streaming from her eyes, down her morose face, while her two children argued over what to watch on their iPad, oblivious to the rest of the world.

There was the elderly man who sat a few seats behind her, with a face of sullen resignation, the face of someone who had lived enough life to anticipate its inherent unfairness—insurance against shattered hopes. And then there was the young man with the Seahawks cap, baggy jeans, and dark hoodie who sat next to me, mimicking a description of any generic black suspect that could easily put him in the crosshairs of a "concerned" citizen's nine-millimeter.

With eyes focusing laser-like somewhere far off, his face brimmed with a visceral rage that could barely be contained. It threatened to sear through his skin and ignite whatever happened to be around.

I knew what his face wore well. It was an expression my own adorned when I was 13 years old. A Seattle Police Department officer handcuffed me and threw me head first on top of his patrol car—ostensibly for jaywalking. The memory remains indelible: him smashing my temple down onto the car's hood, whispering in my ear, "N**ger, I could rape your mother and you couldn't do sh*t about it." I fought as hard as I ever had to hold back tears, not wanting to give him the satisfaction of seeing me cry.

He would continue to come around the Rainier Beach neighborhood with this wry smirk plastered on his face, knowing that at any moment he could harass me and I could do nothing—except think about killing him.

It was such a young age to be fitted with the knowledge that you are a disposable person, for all intents and purposes. Your thoughts, dignity, and virtues can all be discarded because of what amounts to an arbitrary distinction in pigment. Feeling powerless, you suppress your anger (no matter how justified), hoping beyond hope that you aren't the next target—knowing that your skin color confines you to the burden of being 4.2 times as likely to be killed by a police officer than your melanin-deficient counterparts.

But these things can only be suppressed for so long, which is why I found myself in the midst of a drove of demonstrators who had started off in downtown's Westlake Park adding and subtracting to the numbers as they made their way through Seattle's streets, now packing the lobby of the Garfield Community Center to the point that sardines would pity anyone in attendance.

What was intended to be a calm, low-key "Rapid Response" meeting for youth and residents to process what had just transpired two thousand miles away had now turned into a shouting match between event organizers and demonstrators, with the latter demanding the four police officers in the building leave so that they could peacefully assemble.

A kaleidoscope of sound boomed around me. Megaphones blared, "The SPD are killing our children" and "We will not be co-opted by the cops." Voices shouted, "Hands up, don't shoot" and "Get the police the f*ck out of here!"

With local news cameras soaking in the sight, hoping for a slice of red meat they could use to lead off the night's broadcasts, the demonstrators abruptly shifted course, leaving as swiftly as they came. They marched down 23rd Avenue, claiming the Central District as their own, momentarily shutting down streets and causing buses to reroute as they pounded the pavement south toward Rainier Avenue, intermittently chanting, "Black lives matter."

It was a case study in ad hoc civic protest: disorganized, incoherent, and *necessary*. Crucial, if only to bring the required attention to what is happening across this country and inside our city, as much of an imposition as it has become on downtown Christmas tree lightings. For it's sad that it comes as a revelation to most that these protests are not about Mike Brown or parsing his worth as a martyr. Nor next time—and there will be a next time—will it be about any one individual.

Which is why, with as much sympathy as I had for the protesters that night (and with all of the anger I had long held about what it means to be black in this country bubbling to the surface and feeding into theirs), I couldn't help but be troubled. The thought could not escape me that I had been whisked away from something more radical than anything they could possibly engage in that night.

When asked if what they were doing was going to make any difference, Adam Gish, a teacher from Garfield High School who had joined the demonstrators for a small stretch, responded, "No, but what was making a difference was what was going on in there."

By "there" he meant the confines of the Garfield Community Center's activity room, usually reserved for Zumba and Yoga classes. It had been converted to a gathering hall for anyone in the area who wanted to come and discuss how a decision made a world away affected their own.

Earlier in the night, prior to the protestors entering the building, police officers joined residents of all stripes: black, white, Native, Hispanic. Most had never met before, and under normal circumstances wouldn't have chosen to, as they fell far out of the reach of one another's social circles. But all waited their turn to be heard, to listen, and to unleash unfiltered emotion upon one another. Andrea Brenneke from the Restorative Justice Initiative acted as master conductor, making sure no voice went unacknowledged.

Many powerful stories were shared (several similar to my own), including that of a young mother named Sara who talked about the realization that her children would never be fatally shot by the police because they were white. While the presence of police officers may have felt tense— as a man named Aaron explained, even the 10-year-olds he knew from around the south end and Central District held the mantra, "F*ck the police"—SPD officers insisted that they earnestly wanted to find a way to fix that. But it wasn't what was said that was so radical. What was radical was that it was confronted.

For here in that most liberal of bastions stands a two-ton elephant that stubbornly goes ignored, covered by the veil of "progressive city," and aided in its obscurity by its citizens' predilection for passive aggressivity: Seattle's racism.

There it was, laid bare, staring at everyone in the room without so much as blinking. There was no way around it, over it, or under it. Only through, only head on.

Right then no one could look from an *ivory* Space Needle and wag their finger at those "less" fortunate places that, "just don't get it," or "are so backward as to be laughable." The mythology was shattered that we don't harbor a race problem in a city where the incarceration rate of blacks outpaces that of the nation's. A city where (though marijuana is now legal) blacks are 13 times more likely to be arrested for drugs. A place that, even with a minimum wage increase, is barely affordable for many residents of color who are too often forced to migrate to the city's periphery. A city where we limp along toward police reform while a growing number of residents of color join in the chorus of those aforementioned 10-year-olds.

It was at this point that I saw a hatred galvanize each individual in that room—a hatred that could have so easily been directed at each other—and cinch on a system that many had fallen victim to and others had been ignorant of. Both dispositions now seemed tragic. "America's preferred race" had finally caught up to the mindset of its discarded one.

Ideas began to take shape from the alchemy of collective human imagination: How do we stop this? How do we address this? How do we get those most prominent in an increasingly gentrified city to accept what our city has become—and change it? How do we make sure that this time motivation and action isn't eroded by the diminishing returns of successive tomorrows?

I'm not gullible enough to assume that a handful of people in one room can alter a system that has proven implacable since its creation, nor am I cynical enough to say that it has no impact. Historically, the grandest of ideas begin in a room with a limited number; just ask Karl Marx, Adam Smith, or Paul of Tarsus.

We need more rooms occupied by people who are willing to brave judgment, disdain, fear, anger, and shame—justified or not. We must get to a place where a small group found themselves one fateful night, when the death of an 18-year-old made them hold a mirror up to their city and see that its reflection did not contrast with Ferguson's as much as they would have hoped.

Confessions of an Imperfect Ally

THAT MOMENT WHEN YOU'RE FUTILELY clawing at the boot pressed against your neck as your windpipe collapses may not be an opportune time to notice your own Sorel crushing another's throat, but in today's America it's the ideal hour.

I'm reminded of that almost daily with this country's limitless varieties of oppression: white over black, male over female, cisgender over non-conforming, rich over poor. All of them existing simultaneously, colliding, merging, and morphing into new forms of ever-perpetuating others.

Shouting your pain so people notice means you often find yourself hoarse and unable to lend voice to much else.

And yes, I know the word "intersectionality" has made its long progression to America's buzzword pantheon … even Hillary Clinton used it. It describes the manifold and overlapping social miseries our country doles out depending on your gender, color, or class.

Ironically enough, it's risen to the heights of our national lexicon at the same time that we continue to decry "identity politics," or, in other words, all political issues that do not revert to the mean—America's so-called "common identity."

The instant classic of an argument goes something like this: Instead of focusing on the anti-trans bathroom bills, the ravages of white supremacy, or those other pesky injustices of America, we need to uniformly focus on "our" collective economic fortunes—no matter how unequal those economic fortunes have stubbornly remained throughout history.

White working-class voters did not coalesce around Trump for emboldening racial indignance, so the argument goes, but because of "economic anxiety"—a memo mind-blowingly missed by the POC working class who turned out for his opponent. The rising tide of financial well-being will be high enough to cover all the other inequities, apparently. The unspoken oppression will be left to lurk just below the surface.

I was reminded of this looping narrative not a month ago, while standing in a coffeeshop line. A transgender woman, speaking about the murder of black transgender woman Brandi Seals, began to sob uncontrollably.

"No one gives a fuck about us. No one cares," she said.

It was impossible to argue. I've seen thousands march in this very city for straight, cisgendered black males: Che Taylor, Mike Brown, and countless others killed by police.

I've yet to witness those numbers for any of the 28 transgender people killed in 2017, nearly all people of color (a significant number black and Indigenous). It was the deadliest year on record for the transgender community.

Quite frankly, I can see how easy it is to feign concern with words, but be indifferent with actions to combat the rash of hate crimes against the transgender community—even those committed in our own city.

Our innate American default is to be preoccupied with the me: *my* pain, *my* hurt, *my* struggle, *my* life.

Rarely are we socialized to see how our pain, our hurt, and our struggles, indirectly impair the lives of others.

It was an assessment I was challenged to make recently by community organizer Banaa Be.

Interviewing her for a forthcoming story, I asked her how it was possible for someone to simultaneously "chew gum and skip rope"—that is, fight both toxic masculinity and anti-blackness at the same time.

Probing me as if Serena Williams just begged her advice on how to properly hit a forehand, she politely responded by saying I was better equipped to answer that question.

It was as humbling as it was a profound reminder. In my numerous screeds on the responsibility of society's superfluously empowered and privileged to diminish their positions, I found myself overlooking my own status.

I reflected on a visit to an old family friend's church nearly two years ago. The pastor preached that Black Lives Mattered. He led the all-black congregation in prayer for the families of those slain, whether in streets or crack houses. He appealed to God for mercy for their lives.

However, the "black lives" he exalted soon became clear.

This non-practicing agnostic fumed at the prayer for "those lost people" at the Pride Parade, gritting my teeth as the minister directed the congregation to sign I-1552 (a state bill that would've removed protections for transgender people in restrooms, locker rooms, and homeless shelters) as they filed out of service.

Never mind that transgender people are far more likely to be victims of bathroom attacks. Never mind they are disproportionately murdered as members of the black community. The black minister spun a yarn of fear featuring a transgender person preying upon an unassuming youth to justify his stance, met by a resounding chorus of amens.

At the time, I attempted to rationalize. I said nothing. I did nothing. I just darted through the door past the petition, so I didn't have to bother explaining why I would never sign such a hateful document.

It would have taken too much courage, too much defiance, too much disrespect of my elders and my heritage. That was my rationalization: I'd be betraying the community that welcomed me that day, and with it the fight for justice, and against terror, still raging in the black community. To point out that wrong is wrong, regardless of its perpetrator, would have "drawn desperately needed attention away from" that community's struggle. As if a modicum of concern for the "oppressed, within the oppressed" couldn't be spared.

As a straight cisgender male, I had nothing to lose, not really, in speaking up for those forced into silence.

As heavy as the boot you struggle against may be, its weight can be more than matched by your own squashing the lives underneath you.

WHY AN ATHEIST SAYS AMEN

THANK YOU FOR ALLOWING ME TO SPEAK today. I think it's only at a Unitarian Church where a non-believer can occupy the pulpit without spontaneously bursting into flame. However, if I do happen to get struck by lightning on my way out of here today, you'll know that everything I'm about to say is wrong and you can feel free, for your own safety, to disregard the forthcoming sermon.

I have to admit it's not the easiest thing to talk to you today, for a couple of reasons. For one, I don't think just one person can truly hope to speak for any group of people, and as someone who has on more than one occasion found himself with the unenviable task of having to somehow speak for the entire black population to a few groups of, shall we say, less-than-open-minded people, I can attest to its difficulty. The second reason why it isn't all that easy to speak up today is, well, who in their right mind wants to ever admit that they're an atheist?

Should you find yourself in the company of longtime believers or the recently saved, there may be no more terrible proclamation than, "I don't believe in God." (I'm still here, so, so far, so good). I really wish that that was an exaggeration, but unfortunately it isn't, as recent polls indicate that on average people are actually more likely to vote for a pedophile, a murderer, or a kleptomaniac before they would ever would vote for an atheist for elected office (of course, with the quality of some of the politicians we have in office, that doesn't sound all that that farfetched).

In some states, atheists are routinely denied child custody rights in a divorce, just because of their stated lack of belief. And as of this present day, you can be put to death for being an atheist in several Middle Eastern countries. And then, of course, there's the label of atheist being synonymous often times with immorality—and the malevolent dictators Stalin, Mao, and Hitler (although Hitler was actually Catholic; not that that particular institution needs any more bad publicity). As you may have deduced, being an atheist is absent of most perks, unless you count rampant stigmatization and being associated with evil incarnate.

And while it's true that there are horrible people who happen not to believe in God, as I'm sure is the case with any group, there are also wonderful people who have that label, such as the actors Angelina Jolie and Bruce Lee. So atheists can be beautiful and badass (sometimes at the same time). There are also the billionaires Warren Buffet and Bill Gates, two of the most charitable people on the planet, and to counter Stalin and Mao, we have Dilma Vana Rousseff and Julia Gillard, the leaders of Brazil and Australia, respectively, whose countries have less inequality and more class mobility than even our own. Of course, since both of those leaders also happen to be female, that may be more of a case for women ruling the world than that there are good atheists, but that's a talk for another day.

It's a shame that more of those people don't come to mind when you hear the word atheist. If they did, maybe, just maybe, regular people who work their 9 to 5 wouldn't be so scared of the repercussions they'd face if they said they were. Instead, they're told that atheists aren't worthy of love (according to the comedian Steve Harvey) or that we shouldn't be considered citizens of the United States (according to former president George H.W. Bush. And he's supposed to be the smart Bush!). Atheists should be registered just like sex offenders are, says the renowned Baptist Pastor Mike Stahl, or atheists will spend an extremely long time in the pits of scorching red hot flame for all of eternity, says pretty much everyone who's not an atheist (present company excepted, of course).

It's tough enough to come out and say what to you carries no more gravity than saying, "I don't believe in Zeus or Poseidon," but to everyone else seems to carry heavy social repercussions. It's made tougher still when those words that I just quoted don't just come from celebrities, presidents, or fire-and-brimstone fundamentalist preachers (or, as I like to call them, crazy people), but from people who are close to you, who love you—until they hear the revelation that you no longer believe what they do. There are countless stories of people who have come out as atheists only to be excommunicated and ignored by friends and family. There are people who have been ostracized from communities, and then there are women and children who have come out as atheist and then been violently abused by their husbands and parents, who hope to beat God back into them. If only people who didn't believe in Santa Claus had it this bad.

Thankfully, my own experience with coming out to someone I was close to didn't have that severe of consequences, but it was eye-opening, nonetheless. There was a period in my life that I had decided to become a devout Lutheran. Along with finding God I met a Lutheran priest during this time who became very dear to me and, for the purposes of this story, I'll call him Pastor Steve.

Pastor Steve was a guy who could do absolutely no wrong in my eyes, or pretty much the eyes of anyone else. It didn't matter what time of day or night you needed him; he would drop everything and be there for you. He was better than the postal service. He'd be there for you in rain, sleet, snow, cantaloupe-sized hail, tornadoes, it didn't matter. It seemed that all that mattered to him was you. He'd never judge you, nor get angry with you, no matter how deserving of his wrath you might be. I used to think that he was incapable of saying a cross word about anything or anyone, because the few times I did see him get frustrated, his vocabulary consisted of "aw shucks" and "darn it to heck." If the entire world had turned its back on you, so that not one person would pee on you if you were on fire, you had Pastor Steve who would at least spit on you. I felt that there was nothing in the world that I couldn't talk to him about and I told him things that, to this day, I haven't shared with too many other people.

After about a year or so (when I fell out of love with the girl, of course), I began to struggle with my belief in God and how that belief, at least for me, seemed to no longer conflate with the reality I saw around me. In a world that is sometimes full of immense and horrific suffering, and where natural disasters happen that appear to be indifferent to who they touch, I couldn't find a divine plan. In a world where people, including the ones we love, sometimes die senselessly without in reason or rhyme to it, and where good happens to the worst of us, and bad to the best us, I could no longer believe that there was a benevolent being who had the power to stop these atrocities, but would not. It was difficult to come to these conclusions. Like anybody,

I found it hard to go against the grain of things that I had been taught and conditioned to think for so long. I had been taught and had it repeated that God was everything and without him I was nothing. But I found that when I let that belief go—the belief that there was some almighty father in the sky keeping surveillance over us—that it was less like I had let go of the comfort of a warm blanket only to feel the cruel cold of reality, and more like the experience of a certain cartoon elephant who, when relinquishing hold of his magic feather, found that he had the freedom to fly as far and as high without it as he ever could with it.

As Pastor Steve was a man I felt I could be an open book to, I emailed him about my newfound beliefs, or lack of beliefs, if you will. While I expected him to be a bit disappointed, I figured that he would respond back in trademark Pastor Steve fashion with an upbeat reply, wishing me God's bid. Call it naïve if you will, but I was shocked to get inundated with several emails, the majority of which were in red letters and all caps. This was less "Godspeed" and more "God damn you." Gone was this cherub-like, gentle man; he was replaced by a bitter Mr. Hyde who didn't just denounce my beliefs, but seemed to denounce me. Our correspondence with each other went back and forth for about a year, getting to the point where, in his responses to some of my ideas, he seemed to miraculously develop a vocabulary of several four-letter words. I didn't know whether I was talking to a priest or a maritime sailor. This seemed ironic, as I was the one who was supposed to be the atheist and he seemed to be the one losing his religion.

Our correspondence culminated in one email that I'll never forget; it actually inspired this talk today. It said:

Marcus, an atheist is defined solely by what he doesn't believe in. The word itself means to be without; that is all it means. He has no compass to steer him so he is directionless in all his ways, no principles to edify him so he will fall for anything, no moral fiber that sustains him so he consists of nothing, and therefore with no beliefs, he is not deserving of the life given to him. His very existence is pitiful, unredeeming, and pathetic, as your entire life is lived as life without, without hope or without optimism, without certainty. It is a pity that an atheist can never say the sweetest words that I am allowed to utter, that affirm his beliefs, as he doesn't believe in anything, the words let it be so, or as a believer would say, amen. The path you are on is a lonely, cruel walk towards a deserving eternal lake of hell fire, and one where you will know nothing but agony, torture, and sadness along the way, but I needn't tell you as you will find this out for yourself soon enough.

With Warmest Regards,
Pastor Steve

Thankfully, I haven't gotten too many more heartfelt letters from Pastor Steve, as we stopped speaking to each other a few months ago, but since then I've had several encounters with others that certainly agree with his assertions. People can never seem to fathom what life is like without one single belief, as if belief is the straw that stirs all others. The thing is, I usually don't correct people when they tell me that I live a life without belief, because they're 100 percent accurate. Indeed, I do live a life without belief. … in a deity.

You see, yes, I am without a belief in a deity who dictates my moral absolutes, because instead I believe that we have the tools that equip us to construct an idea of how life can and should be lived. I believe that these tools include a mind that concerns itself with the community of our fellow men and women, a heart that bleeds with empathy, and a history that distributes a wealth of knowledge from the experiences of those who have come before us. That is why I do not believe that the good of an individual is rightfully measured in proportion to how it appeases some supreme being, but instead measured by a willingness to do good, even when you think no one else might be watching; it is done for its own sake without promise of reward.

And yes, I'm without a belief that what some call "spirituality" and "church" is solely the property of a holy book or building, because while I don't doubt that the claims of people being overcome with a spirit or force are true, I know it's possible to feel the spirit in a church that extends past four walls. We all belong to one: it is the self-transcendence that is found in loving someone as much if not more than you do yourself, as a parent does a child. It's a church where I've seen people overtaken by a rapture they find in the arts—by ears lent to Shakespeare's words and Jimi Hendrix's guitar. It's one full of the euphoria that comes with the passionate touch of a lover's embrace. It's a place where the sheer awe from the contemplation of this vast universe we find ourselves in overtakes us, and where we gaze at the stars at night as their light kisses our faces. It's a church where I've experienced the grace that none of us is deserving of: the true companions in friendship who put up with you many times in spite of yourself.

And speaking of "deserving," like traditional believers, I am without a belief that we deserve this life. That's because when I look at so many things that I had absolutely no control over, such as where, when, and to whom I was born, I see that I don't deserve this life, any more than a child born in Botswana who will not see his fifth birthday because he will be dead from AIDS deserves his, nor more than a young Jewish woman born in fascist Germany during World War II who perished in a concentration camp deserves hers. No, I'm not deserving of this life, because in my genome, or in the genetic material that makes all of us up, there are endless combinations of ways that that material could have come together. The number of people who could have been born instead of me outnumber all of the drops of water found in the ocean. My own genome could have come together in such a way that geniuses that rival Einstein and athletes that are superior to Michael Jordan could have taken my place on my birthday. Yet instead of those people existing, here I stand in front of you, just an ordinary man of very limited distinction. No, I don't deserve this life, but I believe that I can make myself worthy of it, by living not as if it is a marathon or sprint to be endured or hurried through, nor as something to be taken for granted or squandered, but as a unique privilege in and of itself to be savored, treasured, and cherished, beyond measure. Making myself worthy of it by living a life like my grandfather lived: filled with a passionate curiosity and a hunger for knowledge, wisdom, and life itself that could never be satisfied. He lived this through his deeds and actions, too, so that although his life was finite, his life's work continued to echo in the lives of others long after he was gone, so that hopefully people could say that if the pain they felt in their hearts at his passing was the price they had to pay for the love he left, they would have gladly exchanged it for having known him.

I am without a belief that simply stating our hopes in words is enough on its own to solve the trying times we are often confronted with. Instead, I believe that we encounter serious problems in our world and in our lives that demand of us serious solutions; while I do value reflection and contemplation, I don't know of too many problems that have ever been remedied by bowing away from them and dropping to our knees. They are solved by standing up on our feet and facing them courageously, even when we have to strain with every fiber in our being to do so.

I'm without a belief that stigmatizes or segregates us by race, gender, or sexual orientation, as if we are all some subspecies of each other, as if I can possibly assess your worth as any less than my own. So, in truth—and you may find this surprising—I do not believe in atheists, or agnostics or humanists, or Christians or Muslims or Jews or Gentiles, for that matter. Instead, I believe in people: people who want to know that they aren't alone. People who want to know that they are loved. People who have doubts and uncertainty and try to color in the shades of gray this world offers them with black and white. People who sometimes try and fail and sometimes persist and succeed. People who sometimes make mistakes that they can never seem to fix. People who transform their lives with the resolve to do better. People who want so desperately to stand out at times, but want so badly to fit in at others. People who sometimes hurt and get hurt by people they care about with every atom of their heart. People who sometimes crumble in the face of adversity and people who sometimes find the strength to discover greatness within them that they never realized they had. People who are all in this together, and want to know that their life has meaning, and purpose, and that it isn't lived in vain.

And you know what, that doesn't make us sinners or saints; that doesn't make us wicked or wretches or scourges of the earth or debtors who owe a bill that we can never repay; nor does it make us weak or abnormal. What that makes us is human, and there is absolutely nothing wrong with that, nothing.

As it is, there are so many things in this world that ail us, that cause us fear, frustration, anxiety, and despair, such as inequality, racism, xenophobia, senseless violence, poverty, the erosion of social fabrics, and more. And regardless of your beliefs in a deity or lack thereof, we can all agree these things have their beginnings in human beings. But we can also agree that there is so much good in this world that share those same beginnings.

I've heard it said once in a discussion about God that he is an idea that constitutes the best that is inside all of us, the best that we are capable of. That's one idea that I've certainly pondered because as a former President of ours said—a Catholic no less—that ultimately on this earth God's work must be ours. With all respect to Mr. Kennedy, I believe that it cannot stop there, because so too must his compassion, his grace, his forgiveness, his mercy, his kindness, his sacrifice, and his love. I do not believe that those things are ours because it is the will of a supreme being who is claimed to be housed above us, but because it is the choice of those human beings who reside amongst us. And that is a choice that we can make at this very moment, and in making that choice I think that we will find that "heaven" is just another word—a euphemism for a place that we call earth and lives that we call our own.

I must confess to you, however, that the naysayers are correct about atheists, at least in this case, because I stand here without any hope and optimism in regards to that belief. No, instead I stand here certain of that belief. So, you see, there are things that are so worthy of devotion, that are so majestic in their conception, that are so beautiful as to inspire faith that they will come to pass, that no matter what you call yourself, or are labeled as, we can all answer to them with the resounding affirmation of "let it be so"... or, as even a man that people would call an atheist would say, Amen.

Life Before Death

I am going to die. Those words are as plain and bereft of spectacle as one can possibly get, but they rumble with such profoundness. There is probably no other combination of five words, along with their implicit meaning, that we strain to elude more, and yet in a lifetime of avoidance, here I stand accosted by them. When seized by that moment, you begin to understand that immortality is a mere wish that will, like most, go unfulfilled. All the cliches associated with that revelation have the accuracy of a master archer.

Denial, hand-wringing, pleading to a higher authority whose existence is still in contention, the writhing of your insides, and the rupturing of your soul, all act as tributaries that feed into the reluctant resignation to your plight. To be sure, your acceptance is a cold one, without comfort and unfiltered by any delusions of hope that might prove a counterweight to your predicament. No, instead it provides the blunt blade of reality to scrape away such nonsense.

It's a lamentable report that as of right now, there is no recourse from my fate, as there has been absolutely no one to ever recover from it, other than a few alleged cases that remain more folklore than fact, I've been told. No, my ailment is unfortunately irrevocably fatal, a harsh sentence handed down, and if I am to be unrepentantly honest about my past trials, it is more than justified. As I now find myself in transit to a ceaseless conference with oblivion, it orchestrates thoughts of things both done and yet to do, words spoken and held onto, loves lost and preserved.

As I write, I must ask you to forgive my rudeness, as I have yet to acquaint you with the matchmaker for my imminent demise. It is a very enigmatic and mortal condition that the wisest of sages have yet to come close to fully comprehending, if not somewhat approximating. However, in colloquial vernacular, it's known as "Life."

Yes, *that* "Life." The same epidemic that has infected us all, to varying degrees, since the lethal action of our birth. So that means—by implication, dear reader—that we are both shackled to the same fate. As such, I'd advise any sympathy that you so charitably bestowed upon me during these opening passages be returned to you in kind, free of guilt, because there is no chance of survival by any one of us.

Whether the time we have remaining manifests itself in days, months, or years, it is more semantics than arithmetic, as it carries limited leverage over the fact that our being born seals us to some date of expiration. As opposed to the gift that keeps on giving, life more often has the quality of the gift of constant paradox, one that perpetually gives and takes away: our loved ones, opportunities, fulfillment, memories, and finally itself. It often arrives and departs at moments less than prime. Our opinion on this matter merits little, though, as it is revealed time and again that whoever's hands this arrangement is in, they are not ours.

What triggers my thoughts around this rather somber topic? Perhaps a warped fascination with death, or a recent infatuation with a postmodern fatalist viewpoint of our circumstances? *Au contraire.* The spark acutely originates from confusion with the current lack of regard the majority of us seem to possess for life, as evidenced by the banality we accept during the practice of our days.

It's oddly fascinating that our lives are bookended by celebrations—the first during its inauguration, the last upon its conclusion. Rarely, however, do we do all that much, or have cause to do all that much, in between the two. Our slice of life consists of tasteless slabs of tedium wedged between two momentous milestones.

So much for what passes as life, so much of what we accept—the things that prove to be so rote, so conventional in our days—seem to me so remote from what potential exists for our probing. Most days amount to being given full range to explore a grand estate and yet we choose to spend the majority of the time in its bathroom.

The script of life we seem to habitually honor is reenacted day in and day out with very limited variation from our last performance. Days run together, one yielding dutifully to the next, and fail to make any real lasting impression on us. Ultimately this is where we find ourselves, afflicted by monotony, slavishly toiling for eight hours at a stretch, an attempt to unwind afterwards—all to begin much of the same thing again. And we call this "life"? A calendar distinguishing the days hardly seems necessary.

But what else is there, really? After all, as much as we'd love to indulge in our nihilistic impulses, the restraints of responsibility offer not so gentle tugs whenever we've strayed too far down a path of fancy. So it is from the mundane that we take our instruction. The alternative—found in trite idioms that command us to "seize the day" or to "live each one as if it were our last"—seems in constant misalignment with reality when practiced, revealing the sizable holes in this philosophy.

I do have to confess my admiration for that philosophy, though it offers the narrowest of lenses. But what sights we'd be privy to, as to peer through them is to see a display of unrefined hedonism that I'm almost certain would contain moments that would pulse with pure pleasure to the beats of our lives. I can envision savory glimpses of us telling our employers to make a hasty departure to the mezzanine section of Satan's inferno, the pilfering of all known possessions in exchange for the luxuries of a Caribbean paradise, and the deposit of any children we might have on the porch of an unsuspecting stranger.

Gazing from that view, tomorrow would not factor into the equation of, "Living fully today." Of course, the unavoidable speed bump on that road to bliss comes in the form of the eventual conversion of tomorrow into today, and the knowledge that its riches or poverty are owed to the investments of its predecessors. And there, alas, lies the fantasy inherent in that thinking, as truly, what enduring good can come from attempting to satisfy an insatiable hunger in a lone day, only to starve for every other one that follows?

But surely life can't be limited in its offerings, a mere riff on the old remark that you can have any color Model-T Ford as long as it's black. We either subsist on the life of the mundane with sprinkles of highpoints, or a life of a proverbial Roman Candle: a lovely burst, tempered by its rapid disintegration into nothing. Such choices make the decision faced by death row inmates—lethal injection or the electric chair—almost enviable by comparison.

When tasked with such a decision, it's no wonder that most choose a relatively conventional life, one that is more in tune with a whisper than a shout, and nearly as noticeable. Of course, the merits of shouting to the point that you lose your voice seem to dissipate on examination.

And while I do have a deep understanding of why that is, I believe that most of our lives call for a much higher decibel level than they're currently set to.

The true tragedy of life comes not from its end, but from how blind most of us are to the truth that every day we live is a privilege. Life is under no obligation to allow our participation in its days. And yet most of us stand oblivious to it, or at least indifferent. We treat our days more like drops from an inexhaustible well, whose depletion is rarely contemplated, whose rationing is never given much thought, and whose vitality is never understood, until it reaches a point where it can no longer be replenished. It is that view of life that allows us to savagely cheat ourselves of its full embrace.

No, not every day will be, nor can be, the best one of our lives. Nor can it be perpetually drenched in excitement or pleasure. But what every day can be is one that we live—truly live—demanding more of ourselves than a proposal of simple existence. Instead of acting as passive spectators watching a procession of days parade by, constantly clutching and being dragged unwittingly by its circumstances, and given a sentence of life "as is," our active participation can be a choice we make every day.

This living of life happens even on days full of drabness, as it is up to us to find cracks in the facades that allow glimmers of awe to shine through—awe for what it is we are a part of—as brief and as tiny as those cracks may be.

And in recognizing the uniqueness of this experience we do not discard the contents of all those days previously lived, or yet to be. Rather, we arise each morning in the presence of the resolve that possibility is woven within our waking hours, and that who we are, where we are, and what we are can concede to the demands of change.

It's this approach that advocates for our blatant thievery from life, as it houses within it a bounty and yet is very stingy in its generosity. To most of us, it parcels out the bare minimum, we scavenge up crumbs that descend from its table, and that amounts to a life as we know it. To just accept what life offers you is to forever live unfulfilled and malnourished. And that is why the act of larceny from life is a mandatory practice, as, like any oligarch, it does not willingly give its wealth away. This is what makes the moments we steal and the lives we make from them all the more precious. It is this rare currency we can extract carefully from the gluttony of lesser moments that becomes the measure of a life worth living.

It is unfortunate that so few are initiated in this course of action. Most seem satisfied with the alternative—the one where they make due on the bland morsels rationed to them, hoping for the occasional steak to befall them, afraid to snatch for more off the menu than what is arbitrarily allocated to them.

It is this course that puts up meager opposition to the notion that we function on this earth merely as forgettable decoration to the events that persist around us. This path, if travelled for too long, diminishes our ability to distinguish between places of arrival and departure, as the lack of extraordinary landmarks makes it difficult to do so; all seem so eerily similar. Granted, this way leaves you with fewer twists and turns, and its vicissitudes are not quite as severe as they might be otherwise. But why travel the alternative route, when after all, both will lead you directly to the exact same place? There can be no diversion from your final destination.

And it is that which illustrates the true idiom of our lives. How it ends, or that it does, is really of no consequence. It is the course we set off on to see as much as we can, do as much as we can, pursue as much as we can, in hopes of placing our lives' dreams in closer proximity with reality. Life itself looms large and we must pilfer from it all we can.

The length of our lives, when compared to everything else we know about existence, spans but the duration of a breath. And so why not gasp feverishly with it—in all we do, in all we experience—while we can? Because yes, I am going to die, and so are you. That has long been removed from the realm of uncertainty. The only question that remains is, "Will you live?" That question presents itself today, and all after.

"May you live every day of your life." ~Jonathan Swift

When Your Only Hero Falls

THE SCREAMS COME IN FREQUENT, ballistic salvos that slice through my dreams and rip me from sweet slumber every twenty minutes. *"Don't let me fall, please don't let me fall!"* I heard that exact repetition of words so often I genuinely started to wonder if any others persisted in the English language. The shouter is my grandmother, in what was an all too typical pre-dawn exercise. She had developed a phobia of falling anytime she wasn't standing, which, unfortunately, wasn't avoidable for anyone who was as effectively paralyzed as she was. I would rush from my bed to find her frail body crumbled on the floor in her room, unable to avoid what she adamantly protested against.

However, she was never going to admit to needing help until it was too late. It wasn't in her character to allow a little annoyance, like her arms and legs ignoring most of her commands, to deprive her of carrying out the solemn practice she's engaged in since she was a girl of four years old: meeting the sun as it submits its first light of the day. For her, the worst thing in life you could do is "let the sun find you on your back in the morning. Because it'll confuse you for being dead, and that ain't nothing to be." That's unfortunately something she was never quite able to instill in her grandson, whose love of late mornings comes from his *amore* of the late nights a writer's life entails.

For her it was an unbroken ritual that's inherent in the upbringing of a girl who grew up on a farm in Texas: waking before dawn had cracked to slave away at squeezing milk from the udders of cows, so she could make it to school on time, and then, after a full day, she would return home to work in the field, harvest food, cook for the family, memorize a Bible lesson, practice with the church choir for a Sunday performance, complete her homework, and then finally wash and prepare her clothes for the next day.

Though she had been told countless times—since the day my family decided to rotate primary care of her during the week—to wait for one of us to get her from bed, she never did. It was her willful insistence that there was nothing at all wrong with her. It was a theory aided slightly by the fact that her limbs would, on a rare occasion, give in to her commands, albeit briefly.

In some ways, it was fitting, because this stubborn determination had always been my grandmother's trademark, and it was the only thing in her final days which resembled the woman who helped rear me. Everything else about her had the bearing of a stranger.

The extremely lucid, witty, cogent woman I knew growing up became barely recognizable in the person who for the past year barely remembered her name, or mine—as I had been everything from Marvin, to Jimmy, to Lenny, to Betsy—or the person who carried on constant conversations with dead relatives who she would make dinner dates with, then turn irate when they failed to keep the appointment. It wasn't long after that she began to complain about three men sneaking into her bed with her at night. She accused me of running a brothel, screaming that she didn't want to be "taken for a promiscuous Jezebel."

It was more than just dealing with her hallucinations that made it a hard struggle; it was also the constant assault on my self-esteem: cooking meals that were never good enough (as a man whose culinary skills span the scope of buttered toast, I can confess that they aren't), changing diapers that automatically initiated my gag reflex as the funk that dispelled from them was enough to tear the paint from the drywall in her room, and lifting all her weight that was as static as any cadaver's, all the while being treated to the incessant ditty of, "You can't do anything right!!!"

It was one that was sung to me just the other night as I vainly attempted to adjust her pillow for four straight hours until I could find a position that made her comfortable. It of course turned into an impossible feat that was in no way aided by being accused of attempted murder, as everything I did placed her in constant misery (at 3:45 a.m., she was far from the only one). When I finally surrendered and retreated back to my room, it took all of five minutes until I was back in hers, scrubbing the bed and shampooing the floor, as her bowels had exploded their contents all over, leaving no crevice untouched. My diarrhea-soaked socks can testify as much.

My trials with my grandmother confirm to me the thesis that it's not so much death we fear as *dying*: that point of realization when you accept all the living you're going to do has been done, and you've resigned yourself to wait for that inevitable day you no longer make up a statistic in the census. It's that state where you're no longer talked at, or about, or even to, just *over*. "*What is she thinking?*" "*What does she want?*" "*Why can't she sleep?*" And while the soon-to-be-departed is often in the room while these things are being said, they're now just an ornament of life, waiting for their season to pass.

When my family became aware that my grandmother was living her last days, we knew we wanted them to be spent amongst family, instead of with strangers at a rest home. I remember touring one before we decided to rotate care of her, where so many of the elderly I saw along its corridors had faces branded with this bare, but knowing look, as if in total acceptance of that fate. The appearance was that they had long since passed life by and were now just waiting for it to catch up to them at the finish.

We wanted our goodbye to be as long and as pleasurable as possible, and while long, pleasure seemed to elude us. This past year's constant cocktail of sleep deprivation, foul moods, dirty diapers, and twenty-four-seven marathons of the *Trinity Broadcasting Network* was enough to challenge the most formidable bounds of family, along with our sanity.

It was that last additive that proved the most painful of the concoction, not because of my status as a non-practicing agnostic, or because of the absurdity of commercials for "spiritual testosterone enhancement therapy" that were so innocuously sandwiched between the pleas of charisma-vomiting, rooster-haired, cheap-polyester-costumed preachers for *love* offerings, which they gladly exchange for the answering of prayers (well, not entirely).

It was that it caused me to witness the calls my grandmother made to her God every day while the television was devotedly turned to *His* station, asking Him why He wouldn't *deliver His faithful daughter of the excruciating agony that wrenches every part of her*, and since He *must have his reasons,* why wouldn't He *just let her die?* Why couldn't He please *just take her away?*

It took all the love I had for her, and a few sips of the Johnny Walker Black I store in my liquor cabinet, to quell my incredulity and follow through on her many requests to call one of the scads of numbers that blare on their programming and promise healing of whatever affliction you might have—after you've given your credit card number with expiration date and security code, that is. It took even more to keep from laughing as I found myself on the line with a young, pious telephone operator whose solemn voice cracked every other sentence. Per her instruction, I allowed my right hand to hover over my grandmother as I recited healing affirmations over any part that troubled her (her entire body), while I used my left hand to apply *anointing oil* (Suave Cocoa Butter) to those same powers. All the while, the power inherent in the holy spirit transferred from where the operator was seated in Texas to my grandmother's body in Seattle, Washington.

My attempt not to snicker failed miserably as I hung up the phone and watched my grandmother attempt to convince herself that she felt better. The pain, of course, never abated, although the appeal of a belief in a higher power once again revealed itself to me. It's those moments of absolute desperation, when there exists nothing you can possibly do to unburden a loved one's loss, pain, or reality, that you hope that maybe, just maybe, there *does* exist some celestial being who answers requests at his leisure. For some, it proves to be enough snake oil masquerading as hope to temporarily get you through the day.

However, from what I've seen, if a God does exist, he seems to hide in the most blurry of silver linings. *"Well, at least she only has pancreatic cancer! Just imagine if along with it she had The Bubonic Plague, colon cancer, and retinal deterioration with skin lesions that would leave her sensitive to all manners of touch! Okay now! Praise the Lord!!!"*

Caring for my grandmother was an ordeal, yes, but one well worth undertaking, as no word crafts my image of her more than hero, my hero. But the word, in its contemporary form, no longer does her justice, as most of the gloss that once coated it is gone. Of course, when you attach it to every acid-brained celebrity buffoon, or to politicians who talk out of both sides of their mouths so they can screw you in that one place of your posterior, or when you lavish it on murderers who could have avoided the altercation that killed their victims, what else could be expected? It's inevitably dull.

It's a shame, really, because it was once reserved for those rare gems life gave us—those people who summon the courage we wish we possessed ourselves, and who act in ways we dream of acting, but for one reason or another cannot. It's this word, this simple two-syllable, four-letter word, that used to be laced with so much meaning, that truly describes my grandmother.

It's this woman who, when I was nine years old, stopped in the middle of cooking dinner to calmly load her shotgun, as if it was her garden's seed dispenser, to protect the grandson who had just blown into her house to hide from gang members who had been terrorizing the neighborhood. They were non-discriminatory in putting young and old alike in the hospital. While everyone else locked their doors, she walked from hers, her flowery apron accessorized by a double-barrel, and announced she would "kill every last one of you motherfuckers if you dare lay a finger on my grandson's head." With my heart racing and hers at a mellow beat, she returned to fixing supper while my pursuers made themselves scarce and asked, "Are you hungry?"

That's the indelible impression of my grandmother I'll always carry. There was never anything life could concoct that she couldn't abide on her own terms, or amend with some straining of her will. It's this woman who I never saw cry, no matter how many of her siblings and children she placed in graves, and who I never saw admit to pain of any kind, no matter how tormenting. It was her demeanor that seemed to feed so generously into the juvenile notion that we have of our heroes: they are infallible, and therefore incapable of hurting to the levels the rest of us do. It's impossible for them to be like us—to be weak, to fall—because then who would we have to lean on? Who else would cushion our descents?

But fallen, sprawled on the carpet, with her limbs contorted in all but the most unnatural positions, is where I would find my grandmother most days. I would pick up her delicate body and deposit it back into her bed, but I'd always be halted by the fragile pleading of, "Please, just let me stand to see it."

She would say this as her eyes caught a peep of the first rays of the sun that inaugurated the day. It was a small victory to defy her condition by continuing the habitual practice she had done every day of her life, but could no longer do on her own. It was amazing to see how everything else can wither away in a human being, the mind eroded by time and dementia, the body crippled by disease, but the spirit, the will to live, to let life know it still has to account for you despite its stern dealings, can be so resilient as to never wane.

That was why every day I held her sickly body in my arms, as tightly as I was able without breaking her bones, and I did my best to straighten her, while her knees buckled, limbs remained lifeless, and all of her 170 pounds went limp. I strained so hard for her to meet with her frequent morning companion that I developed painful back spasms, but it was all worth it to see her face peel a smile—the only time it ever did anymore—and feel with my heart the return of the woman I once knew. I would always promise to never let her go, never let her fall, no matter the struggle I had to endure, as her body would begin to wilt, my hand searching for something to hold onto.

It found itself in hers this morning, as I sat by her side in the emergency room of Highline Hospital, repeating to her that I loved her, while they removed the artificial breathing apparatus from her lungs. I closed my eyes to count the last of the breaths her body would ever consume, and as I did a flourish of moments flooded my head: advice I wish I would have taken from her, the many of life's blows she softened for me, and the love she freely gave that remains mine to keep. These are the moments that made up her life, the significance of which didn't stop with her breath, nor even when warmth had long abandoned her hand. The hospital chaplain placed his hand on my shoulder and whispered, "Son, it's finally time to let her go."

To Young Storytellers of Color

In addressing you today, as a fellow journalist of color, the most important message I can relay to you is not how critical journalism is to you, but how critical all of *you* are to journalism. I want you to know how powerful you are in this new media landscape where the tried and true is daily being replaced by the new and innovative, where there are no longer any exclusive gatekeepers to information, just trusted sources of it.

And I want you to know that yes, diversity is important, in our newsrooms, printed pages, and on-air talent; and yes, it is important that our media better resembles our population. But diversity, quite frankly, is not enough. You see, I share the same fear that many journalists of color have who believe in our industry. Much like other industries claiming to harbor the best of intentions, journalism uses the word "diversity" synthetically, similar to how politicians use "liberty," "freedom," and "justice," words barren of any authentic meaning when the time comes to take action.

The call for diversity in our news industry today has persisted just as stubbornly as its composition: more than 90 percent White, and 63 percent male.

And yet the response to this plea for diversity remains just as stubborn. The media usually responds with a variation of "we know we have a problem" or "we're trying" or "we're committed." But those words rarely produce equivalent action.

Don't get me wrong; I'm all for diversity, but diversity without addressing what rots the core of our society, and by relation, our news media, will produce only the minutest of improvements.

Because our media, in its everyday coverage, just like our society, is dominated by a narrative that centers whiteness. The experiences of the dominant (read: white) group in our society are taken to be universal, empirical reality, and a baseline for how others are to be perceived and evaluated, even as it masquerades as objectivity.

Media, like most of our country's systems and institutions, is a structure of power for, dominated by, and founded on a supremacy of whiteness. It has been used as one of the single greatest forms of oppression, controlling how communities of color are viewed, and how those communities at times view themselves.

This supremacy manifests itself openly when people of color are presented as caricatures rather than fully-formed human beings upon their deaths. It manifests at times when the worst of them is put on display as a way to demonize an entire ethnicity for the faults of one, or worse, when their concerns and plight are met with silence until it is too late, such as the case in Flint, Michigan. So, to be heard, they have to scream loudly about their community's circumstances, reminding everyone that indeed their lives do matter, whether the media believes this to be the case or not.

A sprinkling of black, brown, yellow, and red faces will do no more to dull the potency of the problems inherent in the media's structure any more than having a predominantly Black police department in Baltimore has ended racial discrimination and police brutality in that city. Because it does not matter how many tokens any industry has, they alone will not summon up enough change at media organizations whose default is the cultural hegemony of one group, and who have no willingness to turn the scrutiny used in their reporting upon themselves to ask how they may be perpetuating a racist system.

It was made clear to me a couple months before I started my publication, the *South Seattle Emerald*, just how dangerous the news industry's lack of introspection is. I was doing a freelance assignment gathering comments about what residents of South Seattle liked about it.

I'll never forget a young man I bumped into in Rainier Beach, on the corner of Henderson and Rainier Avenue.

His response to my question about what he liked about the South End was: nothing. It was the same response he gave after I asked him, "Well, what do you like about yourself?"

"Nothing," he said again, because "they never say anything good about me."

The "they" in question for him was our news media.

He had seen too many times in his area, predominately composed of Asian and Black people, the media come to cover a car chase that happened in the middle of a community parade, but never the parade itself.

Too many times he'd seen the media depict someone as the one exceptional person of color who achieves some sterling accomplishment, but never the people belonging to the community who year after year after year had shaped and modeled the savant.

Too many times he'd seen the media cover the death of a friend as just another statistic, as just another cadaver they called a convict, felon, or rapist, no matter how long ago that was, free of all context that composed the rest of his friend's life.

And perhaps it's naïve of me to believe that had our media actually said something good, something that served as a positive reflection of him, that that young man would still be alive. He died—killed in a shooting related to some petty robbery—believing he was nothing.

Perhaps it's naïve, but I've always wondered, because you learn in this business that people live in the narrative they are told about themselves.

I can't tell you how much the everyday, "ordinary" story that someone either sees, or does not see, impacts their life.

And maybe our media is not responsible for his death, but there is a crime that they are culpable of every day. That is a death of imagination, an erosion of trust, and an apathy for people in our city who continue to be swept towards its margins.

In just this past year alone, I've seen reporters dismiss the concerns of some within the Asian diaspora, suggesting that somehow the category of Asian masks the health and financial disparities that many people in the Laotian and Cambodian communities face. "They're the model minority," they joked. "What more do they want?"

I've also seen a murdered African-American man treated worse than his killer in a story. And I've seen newsrooms, when pressed to reflect on the insensitive way they covered a musician of color, dismiss her essay about their treatment of her as a mere publicity stunt.

Our media is the most important organ of our society and therefore our democracy. When it functions incorrectly, so will and does our society and our democracy.

As many mistakes as the founders of this nation made in crafting the country, a truly free, truly probing, and truly curious press was one of the great things they got right, which is why it is the only industry listed in our Constitution.

Media can function as a corrective in our society. Like any human endeavor, it will never be wholly just, fair, or egalitarian, but it can be better; it can be superior to that what has come before.

Our media is a mechanism we use to help solve the unnatural and stubborn power imbalances that exist in our society, due to wealth, due to race, due to gender. It is the one place that, yes, we must speak truth to power, but we must also speak that truth as loudly and as profoundly to those who increasingly feel powerless. Journalism is where the rich share equal footing with the poor, where the weak are an equivalent match for the strong, and where the marginalized can occupy the core of civic discourse. It is the main transmitter of ideas about who we are, but more importantly, about the possibilities of who we can be.

It is supposed to be a mechanism, yes, for diverse perspectives and opinion, but it is, most of all, a tool of equity, a role it increasingly fails at.

And that is truly a shame because every day we need journalism devoted to producing the stories of people who don't look like us, think like us, dress like us. We need their own voices to speak about their own lived experiences. We need to learn that in an open society, in this experiment we call America there is no better, no worse, but only different—wonderfully, stunningly, equally different—and that difference is to be treasured, protected, and promoted.

It is our media that has the obligation to show us that the shade of humanity we find foreign in others, though it may appear strange and distant to us, is actually indistinguishable from our own.

It must be journalists of color who lead a new movement within our media that does not just press for, but creates, equity in our industry, because those communities continue to be impacted and perniciously affected by a media that just either cannot or will not get it right, to the point, it seems, that many in it have simply given up attempting.

It must be those journalists of color who take it upon themselves to collectively usher in a new era in our media, complete with a new structure dominated not by one group, but shared amongst many, and where a competency of culture and context is not an expectation, but a requirement.

I know that I'm asking a lot from the journalists of color here today. I know I'm asking a lot of you as young men and women, but I am asking you, Ahlaam, Mohammed, Rhea, Jasmine, Merdie, Jaden, and Starla.

I ask you that you not accept this industry as it is, an industry where many times you'll be the only person of color, unfairly tasked with speaking for your entire community, feeling the anxiety that comes always with the decision between adherence to a company line out of fear of reprisal or speaking your truth as a person of color.

I ask you to fight every step of the way, because you must fight. This is how change happens, from people pushing it to be so. The narrative of our society can change if you wish it.

I already know this power resides in you because you are here today. It resides in you every time you step in a classroom, newsroom, or on a sidewalk to report.

I ask you to lead in creating new organizations, new platforms, and new media because as the old media crumbles—or seems to commit suicide by Donald Trump—there will continue to be space for new journalism to step in. There will continue to be holes to fill and opportunities for you to lay claim to a media and its power that others will lay down willingly because it will no longer be an effective enough business model to provide a return to shareholders.

You have the power to create a media that is robust, that elevates humanity over the sensational, and that replaces a system of white supremacy with one that is truly multi-polar, where diversity is no longer talked about but embedded, and by doing so you can usher in a world as it can be and should be.

Most of all, you have the power to tell the truth about your communities, from your communities, and telling the truth can be a revolutionary act of kindness, compassion, and hope, an act conspicuously missing from our media today.

I hope you never doubt that power. I hope no matter where you go, you remember that, because there is a vast world of young men and women who are starving to hear and see something that resembles life as they live it.

A Ceaseless Cry

I WENT TO FIND COMFORT. But I could locate only a tragic familiarity.

Thursday night's vigil for Philando Castile and Alton Sterling, in Westlake Park, had all-too-familiar words spoken, all-too-familiar tears shed, and an all-too-familiar script with characters cast in all-too-familiar roles of black victims and panicky police officers.

I could barely hear André Taylor, the brother of Che Taylor, who was fatally shot by Seattle police months ago, express the need for police accountability and sympathy for the 135th and 136th African-American males killed by police across the country this year.

My deafness had little to do with the television helicopters hovering overhead, drowning out many of the speakers for the 20 minutes I stayed at the gathering.

No, it came from a cry that roared throughout the day from Seattle's black community, a cry of hopelessness, anger, and fear shared with so many nationally for so long. A cry that recognized yet another public demonstration in response to a national epidemic of police violence as nothing more than ineffective group therapy.

It was this screech that made me leave the vigil just minutes after arriving. I suffered incredulous stares of disappointment at what appeared to be my abandonment of a show of solidarity against police brutality. I couldn't stay.

The cry was too loud. It overwhelmed the calls of "not this time" by demonstrators poised to march through the streets of downtown Seattle due to another black victim. I was certain to catch the replay whenever the 137th and 138th African American is killed under suspicious circumstances.

The cry responded with, "I've heard that one before."

It bounced from the walls of the bar I found myself at soon after leaving. The venue provided necessary medication for the pain pulsing through me as I thought about the state of our country and as I saw two other black males toasting the deaths of Dallas police officers killed by a sniper. "Chickens had finally come home to roost," they said, glasses clinking in celebration of death.

The cry raged: "When people believe the law can no longer provide justice, they will seek it themselves."

It began rumbling earlier in the day after I received a text message from a friend. "Wow ... **Another one**," it read. Only a day had passed between the deaths of Sterling and Castile. Two more names added to an ever-expanding list of blacks killed under suspicious circumstances by police.

I attempted to process everything with Dominique Davis, a mentor who runs a gang-prevention group called the 180 Program.

A dozen others had already visited his office before me. All of them shared their fear of living in Seattle while black.

Anger scarred most of their faces as they recounted interactions with the Seattle Police Department, whose officers, they said, had handcuffed them and punched them in the face with impunity. In one case, a man recalled, an officer had said, "I wish you would run so I would have reason to shoot you."

This reminded me of why, even four years after a federal consent decree to address racial bias in policing in Seattle, trust in law enforcement remains unchanged in the city's black community.

Mistrust first seeded in me during an encounter with a police officer in 1994, when at the age of 13 I was stopped for "jaywalking" while coming home from the store.

The white officer handcuffed me, smashing my face down onto the hood of his patrol car, his breath reeking with the smell of stale coffee as he told me, "Nigger, I could rape your mother and there's nothing you could do about it."

I stood in the middle of the street, trembling with horror after he uncuffed me and drove off without another word.

For almost a year afterward, he would smirk at me whenever I would walk into the doughnut shop with my mother, his sinister smile triggering a rerun of the experience. My face would turn away from him, toward my mother. My mandate was to protect her, which led to thoughts of his death by my hands, if only I could get away with it.

Reflecting on my own history, I felt no surprise at the conclusion many of the men who spoke to Davis came to as they called out the names of Tamir Rice and Trayvon Martin: "The only way they'll stop killing us is if we get to them first."

The cry returned to say: "We've lived too long in the land of make-believe in this country. These are not aberrations.

This is systemic. It always has been, and always will be unless something changes, and changes soon."

The cry demanded a response, any response that was not another regurgitated platitude peddling "love, hope, and prayer."

For the cry, there is no amount of hope, nor love, nor prayer, that can satiate a craving for equal legal footing

The cry, if unheeded, will continue to allow fear to expel us from the ranks of sanity, consuming us all in a blaze of hatred.

Ignoring the cry's clamor has already claimed the lives of countless black bodies. It just claimed the lives of five police officers.

I fear this will be just the beginning, not only nationally but in this very city, which despite its liberal sugar-coating has deep-seated issues of racism just like any other.

The cry will continue, piling up casualties as it grows louder, more hostile, and untamable unless taken up by all in this country, echoing a demand for something that has eluded too many of America's racially oppressed for too long: justice.

Searching for Identity in the Land of the Free

For the last year, America has been in the throes of increasing internal conflict. But this country has long been suffering from an identity crisis, since just before the ink dried on the first sentence of the Declaration of Independence.

Who can claim this nation as a land of opportunity? Who deserves its freedom and liberty? Who is subject to its justice? Whose humanity is affirmed by its laws? Whose voice is amplified? Whose is muted?

It's a shame such questions continuously confront a nation so ill-equipped to handle the burden of self-examination. As Alexis de Tocqueville long ago pointed out while documenting our infant country, Americans can do simplicity quite well; grappling with nuance, not so much.

This wrinkle plays into our society's preference to view this nation's role as that of an undimmed light in the theater of human history.

We'd rather forego any critical collective appraisal of our past's hand in producing our present's harvest of national polarization, deep-seated mistrust of our institutions (and each other), and our societal inequities.

It's the reason an increasing number of us have little recognition of the America our fellow citizens dwell in. And no, I'm not referencing the rural enclaves that the media rushed to cover after the 2016 election. I'm speaking to the psychological terrains of what it means to be a woman, impoverished, a person of color, transgender, and elderly in this country.

These lives exist near a wavelength and along a spectrum still unseen by too many. Much too often we'd rather view a manufactured version of the United States that plays out like a Disneyfied version of a Brothers' Grimm fairytale—discarded of all its untidy parts in favor of happy endings carrying the message that no matter what came before, all is well.

It's this version of America still holding much of our civic imagination captive; it's replete with the message that with a bit of "grit" and hard work, all is obtainable, no matter the systemic barriers. The last can be first, the feeble turned dominant, and the powerless transformed into the mighty.

It's this America that greets Black football players kneeling with confusion, mass protests of police brutality with derision, and rampant reports of sexual assault with dismissiveness, unless any of this satiates a craving for celebrity news.

It's a version of America that persists even after *that* election providing a traumatic shock for many, but sadly, little vision for a way forward.

Those "resisting" our current administration may offer opposition, but scarce on the menu is a new way of life or a re-imagining of the mechanisms guiding this country. To too many, Trump comes across as an aberration, not an inevitable reckoning for a society in radical need of reflection and an uprooting of its mythic fables so as to leave a flagrant truth.

Instead we hear that America is a strong nation that will weather the storm. Indeed, ours has been a powerful nation. It has been a wealthy nation. It has sometimes been a generous nation. But has it ever truly been a great nation?

It cannot be until we acknowledge the truth of who we were and are. It cannot be until we actually agree upon exactly what that truth is.

It certainly won't be if we continue force-feeding our citizenry a version of America fueled by fantasy, and if we resort to anger whenever one of our fellow citizens can no longer stomach swallowing such fodder and decides to speak out or take a knee.

Great nations sacrifice comfort for honesty, myths for reality, and coerced uniformity for a revered variety.

No, America is not a great nation, and it was not before Trump. But it can be after.

It first must start with a vision of an America with new values, new principles, a new understanding of our common good, and a new meaning of what it is to be American.

The American character has been associated with many things; one we must lift to prominence is its aspirational nature, a pursuit of being better than we are.

America will always be scarred by the sins of the past. We cannot forget the genocide that accompanied the country's expansion, the slavery that fed the economy, or the subordination of women that persisted throughout its growth to a global superpower.

America can still be great. But there is so much we must shed: our current president, our racism, our patriarchy, our structural inequality, our predatory capitalism, our military industrial complex.

That will happen only if we demand it, every single day of our lives, and if we view the present as fertile ground to grow the harvest to come from our efforts.

There is no moral arc in our universe that naturally bends towards justice; there are only hands that drag society by the collar, kicking and screaming, into a just and equitable dawn.

Those hands belong to us.

BLACK LIVES, WHITE MARCHERS

THE CRIES RANG OUT IN UNISON throughout Seattle's Central District.

Black Lives Matter!!!

And as my own voice joined the chorus of hundreds of other marchers, one next to me gave a heavy sigh.

"You can't go anywhere in Seattle without white people," it said. "Seriously, why are all these white folks here?"

Treading through the CD, we scanned the crowd, taking in the proportion of black to white, feeling every bit the minority in a city two-thirds Caucasian. We were buoys of Hershey afloat in an ivory sea.

Just a year before, it was a different scene. At a march following the death of Eric Garner at the hands of the NYPD, the streets were filled with members of the city's African-American community making a formidable public showing of solidarity against police violence. It was a galvanizing moment early in the Black Lives Matter movement. And, yes, smatterings of white allies were present, but they appeared in a supporting role.

In a very short time, the tide had turned toward crisp irony. Here was a BLM march with a majority of white participants ardently shouting about how much "Black Lives Mattered" in an area that "black life" had been forced to abandon due to high rents and low prospects.

That was almost two years ago. The catalyst for the march was the deaths of nine congregants of Emanuel African Methodist Episcopal Church in Charleston, South Carolina. Those innocents had been slaughtered by Dylann Roof, a domestic terrorist who wore his white supremacy on his sleeve. And while of course these white marchers did not share Roof's politics, and though they meant well, the overwhelming whiteness of the march inspired in me a deep cynicism that poisoned the well of communal warmth. I wondered how many of my white kinfolk were in attendance to simply build their personal brand, this event simply another addition to their "Social Justice CV," along with #BLM Facebook profile pics, effusive Obama sycophancy, and platinum membership to the Ta-Nehisi Coates fan club, all accentuating how "not racist" they were.

Here were hundreds of them flooding past an area once 70 percent black, now less than one-fifth black and "85 percent Black Lives Matter placards," to quote a friend of mine.

That was the last time I deliberately pounded pavement at an organized Black Lives Matter march in Seattle.

I stopped covering BLM marches as a journalist, as well, having grown skeptical of their efficacy.

I do still scroll through the photos, tweet streams, and personal accounts, one blending into the next. What I see are more white faces and fewer black ones. In the past year it has become even more difficult to discern between a march for black lives and one meant to fight climate change or "Impeach Trump."

At first blush, this development might be cause for jubilation. "Isn't it glorious!" the conventional wisdom declares. "White people are woke and getting it in Seattle."

But are they? And what are the impacts of Black Lives Matter marches where the black lives actually present are outnumbered by white lives?

Could this new dynamic actually be doing more harm than good?

As organizer of the largest Black Lives Matter marches in Seattle since 2014, Mohawk Kuzma has had a front-row seat to the transforming demographics of the BLM movement. He says that my eyes are not deceiving me. There is a noticeable increase of white marchers, one that he says signifies that white Seattleites' long hibernation on Black issues is at its end.

"The reason BLM marches are getting more white is because more white people are waking up and seeing the covert segregation and racial injustice and racism," Kuzma tells me. "We see it on the news every day across the nation."

He draws a connection with the overt displays of racism, from pervasive police killings of blacks to the recent domestic terrorist acts by white supremacists, most recently a school shooting by one in New Mexico.

Kuzma says that when he began organizing, he welcomed whatever race, gender, or orientation felt compelled to attend, as long as the marchers understood "that all black lives matter and racial injustice, police brutality, and racism needed to stop."

However, he also recognizes that the increased numbers of white folks are a double-edged sword.

"More white people also brings white ignorance and white fragility," he says. "White people think they have to be respectful during a protest. Sorry, but we as black people don't get respect from anyone, including white people, so why should we be respectful. We are here to get stuff done."

According to artist, educator, and black community organizer Jerrell Davis, the issue of white people showing up to march is subordinate to what's actually facing the black community: black survival. It is a very real concern in a city where more and more black residents are moving to Kent, Des Moines, and other areas of South King County.

"What does it actually mean?" he asks, repeating my question regarding the increasing participation of white Seattleites at BLM marches.

"Does it mean white folks here are more empathetic? Does it mean they're more willing to go to a march they know will be protected by police?"

For Davis, more white marchers equates to an increased police presence at marches. The aura of safety reduces the risk of attending, he says, which leads to nothing more than a march serving as a symbolic act for white people, ultimately leaving the racial status quo unchallenged.

"Honestly that shit doesn't shift the culture of this city," he concludes, his black locks flowing from beneath his green cap.

Davis—who is becoming well-known for his socially-conscious, movement-based hip-hop under the name Rell Be Free—has participated in numerous Black Lives Matter marches in Seattle and Philadelphia. And while he sees these marches as a necessity in the broader movement for Black liberation, and an entry point for previously disengaged white people to encounter movement politics, he says more energy needs to shift to the activity between marches.

"[Seattle has] a Race and Social Justice Initiative, but every week there are black people leaving this city because they can't live here. We have a zero-detention policy in place, but they're still building a youth detention center. So what good is white people showing up on their own time, when black folks have little time left in this city?"

He views such policies as performative, much like the red, black, and green of the Pan-African flag that is painted on the crosswalks of the Central District. These measures commemorate a once-thriving community, but they do little to empower those who remain. He wonders if the same is happening when white perpetrators of gentrification march in the streets for black lives.

"It's befuddling to me," Davis says. "It's as if some people march as some sort of social justice penance. But do those same people ever ask themselves, 'You know ... I'm knowingly moving to this place and it's hurting people, so should I?' "

Concurrent with a rise in white participation is an apparent decrease in the number of black people marching for black lives. It's a shift that doesn't surprise activist Amir Islam. He knows first-hand how exhausting it can be for displaced black folks to travel to Seattle marches.

"Some Black activists are burnt out from marches," he says. "You have to think that a lot of the black community has been pushed out to Auburn, Kent, Des Moines, Puyallup even .... It's hard enough to survive let alone get to your own people for a march."

Islam says he gave up organizing Seattle-area marches about the time I stopped going. He says that marches are simply one thunderbolt in the gathering storm needed to ravage societal racism, and he has chosen to focus his energies on another approach: community development work.

He says he is fine with the increased white presence at Black Lives Matter marches, though he is uncertain of their effectiveness.

"Let white people rally, talk to other white folks, and march for the humanity of black people," he says. "Truthfully, though, it's not like they're doing anything radical, like buying up a block of homes to give back to the Duwamish."

Anti-racist whites say they are listening to the concerns of black activists and trying to guard against transgressions while also keeping the door open to more white allies—something that activist Erica Sklar sees as a source of energy for the movement, but one with many potential pitfalls.

"It's two sides to the same coin," says Sklar, an organizer with the anti-racist organization CAR-W. "The reality of Seattle's population means there's more white folks and could mean more exposure, but white folks need a critical analysis of issues."

That deep analysis includes a raw, unflinching assessment of the role racism has played in shaping our present, and where it has placed white people, relatively to non-whites, in this country.

Sklar, who served as a civilian peacekeeper at Seattle's most recent May Day protest, says she has witnessed white people armed with good intentions, but lacking crucial foundational recognition of the social justice movements they aim to serve.

"When you show up the first time [to a march], maybe you don't know who you're accountable to, but you should know by the end," she says. "I think a majority of white folks come to this work with fervor, but not a deep analysis. One of the deep tragedies of race in this country is white people are never told that they don't belong somewhere. So they think they belong everywhere."

Such a scenario played out last April when Black Lives Matter Philadelphia decided to host meetings free of white people so that their members could "come together to strategize, organize, heal, and fellowship without the threat of violence and co-optation."

Cue the apoplectic white liberal fury (along with the expected alt-right trolling). Black people, working on black issues, outside of the white gaze for some reason elicited outrage.

It was a situation where black people were actually asking white people for support in the form of trust. Trust to organize and heal, free from prying oversight.

I've heard it myself many times: the white colleague with the gilded heart who just wants to know what they "can do," unsatisfied with my Taoist suggestion that "doing nothing" is at times more than enough.

"Sometimes, we as white people have to understand that support means leaving a space," says Sklar.

Fellow white anti-racist organizer Carly Brook says the initial burning desire of many white people to attend a BLM march, particularly after a high-profile killing of a black person by law enforcement, is symptomatic of white folks being "socialized to attend to urgency," without the necessary accountability to the movements they're attempting to assist.

"Seattle has a culture of advocacy, but not organizing for advocates; we try to speak for each other," explains Brook, who organizes with the Seattle chapter of white anti-racist group European Dissent as part of the People's Institute for Survival and Beyond.

She says while she's encouraged about white folks becoming increasingly aware of the acute systems of oppression that black folks face, she echoes Sklar's concern about white people not having deeper conversations about what they're truly fighting for.

The stone-cold truth is that in a city where a mayor's race can be won without one single black vote, the social currency possessed by white folks is powerful. Yet, allies must walk a tight-rope between utilizing the privilege society has afforded to them and making sure they're amplifying the work of people of color instead of overshadowing POC efforts. Here too, there is work to be done.

During a coffee meet-up, activist, musician, and organizer Gabriel Teodros told me about the times his anti-racism conversation has been met with curiosity, while that of the attendant white artist was met with moonstruck fascination.

"It's a reality that when you go into a room with a group of white people, they aren't going to pay attention to us in the same way they would another white person, even though we're both saying the exact same thing," says Teodros.

It seems like common sense, but must still be said: It is only by listening to those who have a lived experience of oppression that white allies can understand what they are fighting for. But there is an important role for those white voices as well, says Sklar.

"The reality of Seattle's population means that more white folks could mean more exposure for [anti-racist] issues," says Sklar.

The best way to reach white people, after all, is through other white people. Just look at a couple recent surveys: Nationally, 91 percent of white people have social networks exclusively comprising other white people according to a poll by the Public Religion Research Institute, and 57 percent of whites believe "reverse-racism" is widespread. This is why European Dissent and CAR-W encouraged their members to discuss racism with their white family members during the holidays. It might make for awkward dinner conversation, but it is arguably more impactful than marching in the streets.

"It's going to take a lot of holding people we disagree with close. We must keep imagining it's possible. It's going to take lifelong work," Sklar says, adding that people must also engage in these discussions with co-workers, friends, and clergy members.

Those routine interactions are how societal transformations are nourished. For the black activists I spoke with, the time to do so is yesterday. If marching in the streets helps get more white people out of their social bubble and engaged with black issues, then, so be it.

"The city is engaged in a conversation of who actually gets to live in the city," says Teodros. "You and I are talking in Seattle today, but it could be Kent tomorrow if we aren't doing the work every day to ensure this community stays here."

In other words: start marching, then take further strides.

Patriarchy and Black Lives

MEN GET GLORY. WOMEN GET OBSCURITY. Queer folks get indifference.

While that pretty much sums up most levels of American society, it's readily applicable to the history of black movements. Too many of them have been hijacked by the tried-and-true formula of a mesmerizing male figure—one who oozes charisma and spouts glib aphorisms by the metric ton—ascending to the top slot of civil rights and black movements initiated by women.

That's why in terms of peak movement consciousness, MLK's oratory will always outshout FLH's (Fannie Lou Hamer). Malcolm X's radicalism will always out-revolutionary Clara Fraser's. And today, Ta-Nehisi Coates' genius garners more acclaim than Brown professor Tricia Rose. It's also why James Baldwin's gayness is mostly expunged from his biography. I'm guessing the aforementioned males are ossified in your memory, whereas the female names spark finger-dashes to Google.

The cruelty of forgetting women's critical contributions to movements would be one thing, but the glossing over of the condoning of physical violence done to them is another. It's violence too often excused because of a call for solidarity, most exemplified by the early life of former Black Panther Eldridge Cleaver: a vanguard of the black-liberation movement, inspirational author, freedom fighter—and admitted serial rapist. In his autobiography *Soul on Ice*, he stated that he raped hundreds of black women "for practice." His comrades knew of his atrocities, as well as his disregard for women Panthers, but did a grand total of jack squat. He was "too essential" to the movement and black freedom struggle. Apparently there was no one who *didn't* view rape as sport who could fill his role?

The tragedy of American movements is that—no matter how "woke" or countercultural—once they've reached a certain mass, they revert to the mean of our society: Straight males at the top followed by everyone else in descending order depending on how closely you align with that trait.

And in terms of black movements, I know the very valid reasons for not wanting to address such issues in the light of day. Movements are afforded only a razor-thin margin of error, and to fight among yourselves under an ever-judging and unforgiving "white gaze" is tantamount to treason.

After all, why should we air out our dirty laundry in public?

Maybe because that's the only way it'll ever get clean.

For nearly a year, I've heard rumors and accusations about some problematic behavior by a few claiming leadership of Seattle's Black Lives Matter chapter. But most people seemed reticent to publicly express their concerns. That changed last December. Black Lives Matter Seattle-King County (BLMSKC) officially launched, founded in response to rampant and continued abuse experienced by straight and queer women and trans folks in the local BLM movement.

On January 2, BLMSKC posted its first message to its Facebook page: "Seattle's Black Lives Matter movement* has been plagued—almost from the start—by abusive men who have co-opted the mantle to promote themselves and have derailed organizing & advocacy efforts by berating, diminishing, belittling, and harassing black women, femme, queer and trans people. As a result, many black and POC targets of this abuse have either left this movement or remained on the fringes in order to protect themselves. Until now, they have not had the power or support necessary to address these issues without being further victimized or targeted."

While BLM was founded by three queer black women, BLMSKC claimed some local leaders routinely alienated the queer community. Taking inspiration from the black women who started the #MeToo movement, they would distance themselves from abusive spaces and create empowering ones of their own.

"It is a huge reaction to the marginalized gender— women, trans folk, etc.—being pushed out of these movements due to abuse and not being listened to due to people trying to co-op their hard work. A lot of us are just tired, really," says BLMSKC co-founder Ebony Miranda, who also helped organize Seattle's inaugural Womxn's March.

That weariness also extends to the "performative art" aspects of BLM support. "I kept seeing the Black Lives Matter marches, but that's all they were. People were coming, but they weren't really that informed on who organized the event or how to get involved in a real way," says BLMSKC co-founder Livio De La Cruz.

Outside of simply being queer-affirming, the new chapter is also non-hierarchical (it has an advisory board where opinions are weighed equally), it develops strategic partnerships (members turned down an appearance at this year's Seattle's Women's March because they didn't feel the white-feminism vibe was in line with their values), and it openly sources suggestions via an online survey.

"For me, what I really want to see is the empowerment of people to know that they can enact change, even though these systems were created to prevent that from happening. You still can do it. I do think that King County is big, but it's also really small," says BLMSKC co-founder Sakara Remmu, who formerly worked for the national NAACP.

The group is currently focused on the elimination of cash bail for those languishing in jail simply because they cannot afford the bail fees, partnering with the Northwest Community Bail Fund for a Valentine's Day fundraiser. They've also set their sights on King County's continued construction of a juvenile detention center, sending out an open letter demanding the county invest in alternatives.

And while the BLMKC members preferred to move on from the past, I did reach out to Mohawk Kuzma, the organizer most identified with Seattle's BLM marches. Kuzma said that the accusations of abuse and harassment lobbed against him were "just people trying to bury and destroy four years of [Seattle's] Black Lives Matter Movement." For tangible examples, Kuzma pointed to the critical role his organizing played in pushing for SPD police officers to wear body cameras, and a recent fundraiser for the Rainier Valley Food Bank. He also said that he wouldn't "bend to infighting" that attempts to destroy the movement to free all black people. (The only official BLM chapter listed on the national registry in Washington is BLM Vancouver, but BLMSKC has filed paperwork to be officially recognized, along with articles of incorporation to become a nonprofit.)

The three BLMSKC founders I spoke with said the near future will consist of direct actions, showing up to the voting booth, and renewed civic participation in the streets and inside meeting rooms, whether with County Executives, police, activists, or community organizers. Most important, however, is the groundwork for something new, something that exists in defiance of the patriarchy and misogyny found in our society. That was the onus to create anew, as opposed to attempt to rebuild something that they felt would be forever broken.

As Miranda puts it, "Why fight for something that you don't want in its current form anyway?"

Our Divergent Mourning

THERE's A COMMON MYTH THAT the black community speaks of gun violence only when law enforcement is its perpetrator. That marches, protests, and ad hoc assemblies ignite only after deaths like Stephon Clark's, killed by a Sacramento police officer March 18 in his mother's backyard. Zealous cable-news pundits continue to publicly hawk the stale notion that mum's the word when it comes to the violence they brand as "black-on-black crime," as was the case when Shamar Curry was killed last year in a drive-by shooting at Rainier Playfield.

But no: We cry, we agonize, we rage, we deliberate, we demand justice. We're too often overlooked. That's what I experienced at Curry's vigil last July.

I was reminded of this while watching last weekend's March for Our Lives demonstrations held across the country. As a multiracial and generational procession of students, teachers, parents, and gun-restriction advocates filled my television, I lauded their attempts to claim a corner of reason in the mad battlefield that is our country's gun debate.

However, I couldn't help but think of those victims of gun violence whose plights remain invisible. Whose deaths remain tolerated.

Last year there were 30 homicides in the city of Seattle. Of those, 19 victims were either black or Native. Combined, both races barely crack 9 percent of the city's population, yet they accounted for 63 percent of homicides in 2017.

Our city and county officials meet these deaths with a relative silence, one that became more conspicuous after my friend Latrell Williams was killed last year on his way to a corner store. While his death remains unsolved, babblers in my neighborhood who will never go on the record to media or police—feeling an inherent and historic mistrust of both when it comes to distilling either truth or justice—say it was a case of wrong place, wrong time: a young gang member going through an initiation, needing to prove himself by killing someone, anyone. Latrell happened to be that unlucky someone.

He left behind a son, a mother, kids he mentored, and friends. As one of them, one who also counts himself a member of the media, I remember waiting for any statement from our city or county officials, whose communication teams have no problem rushing out responses to the misdeeds of our current President, the retirement of a valued sewer-maintenance worker, or effusive adoration for our football team.

But nothing came. In a crowded race of 20 mayoral candidates, only Nikkita Oliver mentioned him, briefly, during a debate.

The radio silence wasn't just for Latrell, but for seemingly every black homicide not involving a police officer. A source formerly within the King County Executive Office said that the attitude was "We'll mention it … next time." When next time inevitably came, it was déjà vu.

"When you have a population that comprises less than 8 percent of your electorate, the political calculus is to not make waves or rock the boat by saying anything," says Gregory Davis, managing strategist of the Rainier Beach Action Coalition, a community-improvement organization working a breath away from where Latrell was killed.

Davis agrees that speaking out about such violence might unearth its origins—root causes that most local officials craftily acknowledge, but are reluctant to stare down: income inequality, wealth discrepancies, and widening opportunity gaps within our public school system. If local officials actually addressed these problems, they might be able to claim more responsibility in reducing senseless deaths than national politicians.

A few months ago, I met Latrell's mother Lynda for coffee. I listened as she reminisced about her son. She spoke about the man he was becoming. How Latrell's 13-year-old son still swears he sees his dad on the couch watching the Seahawks at times. And how her whole heart still hurts.

Throughout, she kept saying his name. No one else seems willing to mention it.

A Mind of Carnage

THERE'S NOTHING SCARIER THAN WHEN your mind becomes a cage of carnage.

Your neurons are scorched, leaving them unable to process anything except the overwhelming pain they're enduring. You're enduring.

No appeals to rationality, no soothing words, no pleas for calm can douse the flame; memory, reason, and coherence all suffer the inferno.

I experienced it first-hand early last month. There is nothing that can prepare you for it.

It was my first episode of manic depression since being diagnosed and treated for bipolar disorder a few months ago. And while I thought I had it handled, this episode—mind off the rails, raging down a road without end, gathering fury as it went—made it clear that I did not.

At one point, I bumbled down Fifth Avenue in downtown Seattle guided by my mother's hand, mouthing gibberish but not able to form sentences. She looked on in tears, emotionally immobilized, unsure of what to do.

This is what happens to people like me when we forget the work that comes with a brain like this. When we forget—or decide to ignore—the reality that life with a mental illness must be lived deliberately, and that tending to your own mind must be a constant priority.

In spite of what so many voices may preach, willpower alone is no match for clinical depression. And willing wellness into existence won't make it so.

This is what happened to me. I became sure that I could do it on my own. I had stopped taking my prescribed medicine—lithium and Klonopin—because, while both had helped me manage what used to be severe mood swings and bouts of unwarranted anger, the combination had led to fogginess and poor word recall—two critical career handicaps to a professional writer.

As often happens, I believed I would be better off without the medication. I was feeling good. My emotions seemed to obey the laws impressed on Icarus: "fly neither too high or too low." Without the medication, I thought, I'd be relieved of the bad symptoms.

And then a funny thing happened on the way to eternal mental stability.

I had reconnected with a friend over the course of a month. Perhaps "friend" is not quite the right word. We'd spent a year and a half in an aimless pattern of expressed love (by yours truly), space, and reconnection.

In the intervening time since we'd last crossed paths, I'd stopped drinking, accepted my diagnosis of bipolar disorder, found a shrink, and dipped my big toe in Buddhism. But I'd never put down the torch I'd been carrying for her.

In that month, we re-enacted a highlight reel of our past companionship. We laughed at jokes only we had the access code to, exchanged amused glances while trapped in dull group conversations. She read even the most mundane of my articles to offer support.

The gauzy shade was lifted when I invited her to an event, but she declined, offering an excuse that should have been more of a hint than it was. But then, we suspend belief for the ones we love. Especially in the full swing of mania.

She finally came clean the next day, over text message of all media. She'd spent the day with her boyfriend—her boyfriend whom she had never mentioned when she carefully parsed her words during our meetups.

What do you say?

Here is where the break comes. This is not to say that is was entirely her fault; after all, people with neurotypical brains experience this kind of thing all the time. It hurts and your brain darts. But, off my medication and failing to prioritize my own, individual health meant I didn't have the tools to do what needed to be done.

People with bipolar disorder often suffer a symptom called "perseverating," the inability to mentally let things go. It gets exacerbated when you stop taking your medication, as I foolishly did. But I didn't know this was something I needed to be looking for. I *couldn't* know.

And so I spiraled. As they days progressed, so did my rumination on what transpired. Why couldn't she just tell me the truth when I'd been open with her? How could she expect full credit for late homework?

Maybe it would've calmed down, but, as often happens in life when you're on the ropes, the blows just kept coming. My cousin finally revealed her cancer diagnosis. A shooting happened in my college town—maybe you've heard of it—Thousand Oaks. One of the twelve dead was a friend.

And the next thing I know, I'm bumbling around downtown Seattle, not remembering much except mumbling to friends and, later, being discharged from a hospital for depression against medical advice because life always seems to stream onward.

The day after I was discharged, I officiated the wedding of two dear friends. It was a job that came with the task of writing an ode to love for the ceremony—when all I wanted to do was light myself on fire and skydive out of a plane without a parachute and land in the quality-control room of a scissor factory.

Somehow though, I made it through.

A remarkable thing about the brain is that it can, even in the worst of times, do the job. You can soldier on for a little, but not forever. Eventually, you have to stop. And take stock. And start to repair it all.

You try desperately to explain the messages you sent, the conversations you had, the actions you took. It wasn't you who did that … but, well, it was you. How do you tell someone that your mind has a mind all its own without sounding crazy? From some folks you thought you'd get understanding, instead you get a "godspeed"—a parting gift for going on with the rest of your life without them.

Something I wish someone had told me at the very beginning, when I got diagnosed all of those months ago: You're going to have this condition every day for the rest of your life. You're going to have to make changes. You're going to have to adhere to a schedule, every morning strictly routinized: thirty minutes of yoga, twenty minutes of mindful meditation, ten minutes of journaling about your mood.

And the people who left you aren't evil or villains, they're people. They're people who might care about themselves more than they do you, or maybe, like you just a few years ago, don't really understand the particulars of a diagnosis that we throw around colloquially. So you learn that when the dust settles, you can do nothing but close the door behind the people who chose to walk out. You don't want the ones still standing with you to catch a chill.

Meanwhile, you are indeed standing after the havoc. Ready to move forward. Prepared to survive.

Pandemic Recovery and Gentrification

ON A TYPICAL TUESDAY, THE BENCH at Paul's Customs Cuts in Skyway is jammed with aspiring "Ebony Men of the Year."

But in these atypical times it sits empty, as its proprietor sits at home.

"Every day is something new. You don't know what to expect," says Paul Hinton, who temporarily closed his South King County barbershop after Gov. Jay Inslee, in an attempt to contain the coronavirus outbreak, issued a statewide stay-at-home order.

Pausing from working on a puzzle with his wife and children, Hinton relays recent conversations with and shared anxieties of fellow barbers.

"It's all about how we're going to make it. Some people are doing house calls with regulars, but I'm really trying to follow the governor's order," says Hinton, who grew up in South Seattle near Franklin High School. Though his business started in his old community, he reopened in Skyway four years ago after Seattle rents grew exorbitant. His clients told him daily variations of that story. Many had migrated further south, as he had, in search of affordability.

He views the federal government's recent stimulus package as nothing more than a tourniquet. And the state's expanded unemployment benefits still won't quite cover the $1,500 to $2,000 a week he pulled down.

Thankfully, he has stashed away some modest savings, and his shop's landlord has been understanding, at least for now. "He still has to pay his rent, too, though," Hinton says.

Hinton is more worried, however, about those who were in survival mode before the crisis. "What are people going to do with [the] $1,200 [stimulus check]? It's a direct deposit to bill collectors. I'm all for the [proposed] rent freezes, but also freezes on utilities and increases on food to stop people from trying to price gouge," Hinton says.

Many in Skyway's business core are worried the government relief won't be enough. The mile-and-a-half stretch that runs up Renton Avenue consists of five barbershops and hair salons, discount grocer Grocery Outlet, two casinos (one attached to the area's venerable bowling alley), a bar, a consignment shop and six churches packed into a three block radius.

Other than the grocer and a handful of convenience stores and restaurants offering takeout, most everything else is shut down.

Part of unincorporated King County, the area has long been neglected by infrastructure and economic and public health investments. Tucked between Seattle and Renton, Skyway boasts nirvanic views of Lake Washington, a racially diverse population of 18,000, average real estate prices cheaper than Seattle's and median incomes of $49,104.

Skyway's new King County Council representative, Girmay Zahilay, took to The Seattle Times in February to argue that the community should become "a model for investing in the area without displacing the people who call it home."

"People were struggling before this crisis, and if we don't do something, they'll be struggling after. We know the consequences of inaction," says Zahilay. He sounds exhausted. The council member has been working sunup to sundown, he says, responding to constituents in need.

The coronavirus crisis has magnified stubbornly unbalanced accounts between those with plenty and those barely holding on. The eviction moratoriums, federal cash assistance—sound good for now, but what about later, when this crisis has abated? With a potential recession looming, a record number of unemployment insurance claims and the Federal Reserve estimating that 47 million more Americans could lose their jobs, how much further will the already struggling and marginalized plunge?

Far, if history is a guide.

Major catastrophes may not discriminate, but the suffering they cause lands disproportionately on communities of color. Racial and social inequities are inflamed, and those considered least during the good times remain neglected in bad ones. So what hope do Skyway and other communities around South Seattle have in avoiding what scholars call "disaster gentrification," the crisis after the crisis that has caused displacement in New Orleans, New York, Miami and countless other places?

"It's a good question," says Ardent Victa, a bartender and lifelong Seattleite, whose work has been threatened by the statewide closures of restaurants and bars. "But the longer the shutdown lasts the more I might start looking elsewhere."

And so might others, accelerating the expulsion of the working class from the urban core, which includes large swaths of communities of color, during a time when economic survival hinges either on receiving a guaranteed salary or extraordinary government action.

DISASTER RECOVERY AND THE STATUS QUO

Metal mauled rock as the bulldozer's blade scooped and piled rubble onto a new foundation overrunning old grounds on 17th Avenue and Lander Street, near the Beacon Hill light rail station. The construction will eventually become two- and three-bedroom townhomes priced between $679,000 and $885,000.

The rock-gutting resounded for blocks, an alarm of transformation many longtime residents know woefully well. Now hushed with the rest of the city, the neighborhood's transformation will restart as soon as the world does.

It is one of several neighborhoods represented by Seattle City Councilmember Tammy Morales that may see residents displaced after the worst of the economic downturn is over. And it's a reason she says that responses from policymakers must also consider justice. Otherwise, they risk dislodging vulnerable communities from their native cities at a breakneck pace.

"No one's thinking yet of what recovery looks like, but now is the time," says Morales.

Morales made fighting displacement a central plank of her campaign for city council last year. She fears many of her constituents will suffer the fate of accelerated gentrification and wealth destruction produced in the aftermaths of Hurricane Katrina, Superstorm Sandy and the Great Recession.

It's why she recently spearheaded a resolution calling on the governor and President Donald Trump to use executive powers to declare a moratorium on rent and mortgage payments. Last week, she and fellow Councilmember Kshama Sawant also introduced emergency legislation that would levy a tax on the city's 800 largest businesses. The tax would give 100,000 low-income households $500 per month for four months.

"We have landlords who have tenants who can't make rent, and mortgages that those same landlords still must pay, as tens of thousands of Seattleites are entering a recession—possibly worse," Morales says.

Her constituents' fears are grounded in experience and research. Columbia University's Lance Freeman, a leading researcher on gentrification and displacement, produced an oft-cited model in 2005 determining areas susceptible to both: locations near an urban core; a median household income less than the 40th percentile for the metropolitan area; and housing stock older than the surrounding region.

Morales' district includes neighborhoods checking many of those boxes, like New Holly, which has a median household income of $20,395, four times smaller than the city's average.

A natural disaster is not a recession nor a pandemic, but all have one thing in common: their recoveries are bound to leave already vulnerable communities further devastated.

"Crisis doesn't just reveal inequality," says Junia Howell, an urban sociologist at the University of Pittsburgh. "It makes it worse."

Howell knows the impacts of disaster gentrification well. She modeled the effects earthquakes, wildfires, and windstorms had on King County's wealth disparities between 2000 and 2015. What she discovered is not surprising: The wealth gap between whites and Black/Latinx communities and between homeowners and renters grew following these events.

The model is instructive regardless of whether a community suffers from a hurricane or a virus. The emergency in question is answered by the same approach.

"Our default [in crisis] is we can't worry about inequality right now," says Howell. "That is ridiculous. We keep saying we're helping everyone, and it's really that we're helping everyone we think matters."

Occupying that category? Affluent white people, says Howell.

The reason is that typical municipal recovery frameworks, patterned on federal guidelines, prize the return of the status quo. Welcome news, if you were already prospering. Not so inviting if lower housing values, poorer schools and lower wages were your everyday.

"Most policies are trying to return us to the norm, particularly a white middle-class norm, that doesn't ask who might be left out of these policies," explains Howell.

And though Seattle hasn't been battered by a major hurricane or storm, it can absorb lessons from economic reconfigurations after the Great Recession. That period saw the wealth gap between whites and Blacks in America widen by a multiplier of 13 (leaving Black households $98,000 poorer) and higher foreclosure rates in Black and Latinx communities. Seattle was no exception. Homes in those respective communities were foreclosed upon 1.3 and 1.8 times as much as those in white ones.

If the past is any indication, without any imminent fundamental change, many members of those communities not already displaced likely will be.

In other words, we can't afford to go back to normal, according to Margaret Babayan, a policy adviser at the Washington State Budget & Policy Center.

"People get comfortable accepting things as they are. Now that there's a crisis, with this stress on our systems, we see we've failed that stress test," says Babayan, who also has a background in public health.

AFTER CORONAVIRUS: A LIGHT IN THE DARK?

Because of Washington's regressive tax system, grocery store clerks, Amazon fulfillment center workers, teachers and other working class professionals have paid a larger share of their wages into the tax base used to address the crisis than have billionaires. And the former group—many of whom have been deemed essential in our present emergency—stands to be worse off after it subsides.

Many of these workers fall disproportionately among the 40% of Americans who can't afford a $400 emergency. They also constitute the whole of the state's poorest residents unable to telecommute. Many have to jeopardize their health and that of their families by resuming movement during the stay-at-home order. By contrast, the richest among us, who effectively had a week's head start on social distancing, have halted their movement and limited their exposure. *The New York Times* revealed this movement disparity in a recent analysis of smartphone data.

For Babayan, who along with her colleagues has called on Washington state to enact a fairer tax code, the data is unsurprising and distressing. Not only does it highlight that the working class is at higher risk of contracting the coronavirus, but so too are many in communities of color. She cites an Economic Policy Institute study showing that fewer than one in five Black workers, and one in six Latinx workers, can work from home. And while the Centers for Disease Control and Prevention has yet to release the demographics of coronavirus patients, data from Illinois, North Carolina and Milwaukee County show the virus is battering Black communities the hardest.

A 2019 Washington State Budget & Policy Center report showed how our state's history mirrors patterns found across the country, in which discriminatory housing policies such as redlining, hiring discrimination and racially exclusionary New Deal legislation helped establish the white middle class, while prohibiting wealth accumulation in many communities of color.

"Had we made investments in the social safety net, balanced our tax system with policies like the Working Families Tax Credit, and expanded our rainy day fund by raising progressive revenue, people would be better off," Babayan says.

But Babayan believes there is reason for hope. Washington's recent expansion of Temporary Assistance for Needy Families benefits is a promising step. She also largely supports the recent $2 trillion stimulus bill passed by Congress, which vastly expanded unemployment insurance to cover most who lost jobs, including gig workers and the self-employed. But, she said, it addressed an immediate need, not the system that has proved repeatedly fragile in times of crisis.

"We made our economic bed. Now we're lying in it," says Babayan.

Absent significant federal investment in the most vulnerable communities, we have little hope of unmaking it, especially as local coffers dry up because of decreased business revenues.

King County Councilmember Zahilay says what's needed now is a social safety net robust enough to help people get back on their feet. He lists policies that to him and other progressives have received a resounding endorsement from our new reality: Medicare for all, universal basic income, universal child care, stable housing.

"There should be no scenario where there are housing-unstable people. No matter how we respond to this pandemic, society will fundamentally change for better or worse," says Zahilay.

Barbershop owner Paul Hinton hopes it's for the better.

"As much as I love America, [the] truth about what we haven't been doing for people comes out when you're in desperate need," says Hinton.

He's heard secondhand stories of people considering selling drugs to feed their families if shutdowns are prolonged. "If this goes on long enough, people will do whatever they need to survive. You have to give people hope," he says.

His own hope is for those standing on the other side of advantage to see the thread of their fate as inextricably woven within the tapestry of pain endured by wider society.

Craving optimism myself, I took Hinton's desires to a member of Seattle's tech sector. For two decades, its cup had overflowed while others had run dry.

Kris Kendall lives about two miles north of Skyway near Hinton's original shop in Seattle's Rainier Beach neighborhood. As a Microsoft employee, he knows he's in a privileged spot. He knows if he gets laid off he can find contractor work in the tech sector. And he also knows things must change.

"Going back to the status quo would be a hard sell for a large part of this country. Why spend money recovering a system that's inherently broken and favors one class over another?" says Kendall.

With a cacophony of ideas floating around, he sees now as an ideal time for discussions about reparations for America's historically disadvantaged communities that go beyond simply parceling out ruminative checks.

"If you're underwater with your bills, you're at the same starting point again," Kendall says. "[It's true that] this event really brings out the best in people. But you can't rely on that prayer-chain style of recovery."

Those who suffer worse in a crisis are the same as those who always suffer, because of systemic indifference. The axiom was etched into Kendall's psyche after the Hanukkah Eve storm of 2006.

Pummeling most of Western Washington, it knocked out power to more than a million homes. But five days after the storm, with power restored to much of Seattle, Kendall found himself driving south from Microsoft's Redmond headquarters to his wife's orchestra practice in Renton.

He noticed an odd thing as he neared Columbia City. Incredulously, the power was still out in South Seattle.

He kept driving for miles, deeper and deeper into the dark. It took him a long time to find anywhere with the lights on.

From Si'ahl to Seattle: Does a Wealthy City Owe its First Residents Reparations?

When she speaks, Rachel Heaton's ancestors flourish as they did for millennia, until the 1860s. They flow from longhouses grouped into villages scattered around 54,000 acres of lush marshes near Elliott Bay and the Cedar and Green Rivers. After hunting ducks on the tidelands and harvesting salmonberries in coastal forests, they assemble to feast on the largesse.

"Every time I give an acknowledgement, I intentionally ask people to reflect on what the land looked like—our villages, our people," said Heaton, a 40-year-old activist of Duwamish lineage and an enrolled member of the Muckleshoot Indian Tribe.

Once Heaton crystallizes those images of her ancestral home in her audience's minds, she moves to darker times—times of lies told by white settlers, of Natives forced off the land that, today, makes up the Seattle area.

"Imagine what this land looked like before the concrete was here and the government came in and burned down our longhouses," she recently told a group gathered at the Seattle Center's Fisher Pavilion. "People were forcefully removed so you could reside in this city and exist as you do."

Today, tribal reservations constitute less than 0.8 percent of King and Pierce counties that hold the Seattle-Tacoma metro. Chief Si'ahl signed the treaty that yielded a city bearing his name, but his Duwamish people never received land within it. The river named for them hasn't fared better; it's among the most toxic in the nation.

Heaton, and many others in the local Indigenous community, seek to remind the 99.6 percent of non-Native Seattleites about these involuntary sacrifices, made so one of the nation's richest cities could take root.

Aiding in that effort has been public recognition of Indigenous land at libraries, churches, city halls, bookstores, coffee shops, poetry readings, and happy hours. Some feel verbal acknowledgment isn't enough, and have taken to paying a form of reparation rent. To some Native Americans, these land acknowledgments can jumpstart examinations of the complex relationships between Native nations and the United States. Tribes have traditionally used them when visiting the land of other tribes to show respect; they figure non-Native folks can do the same.

Such acknowledgments, though, are just a primer for a much larger conversation of what is owed to people pillaged of land, and whose official treaty agreements have been routinely violated by the U.S. government. The question of restitution is absent of easy solutions, and brings no shortage of consternations.

"How do you compensate someone for literally hundreds of years of genocide?" Muckleshoot Tribal Council Member Donny Stevenson asked. "How do you assign some monetary value to lands that have been sacred for thousands of years?"

Growing up in near-poverty in 1980s Seattle, Mary Mathison, 45, credits the color of her skin with lifting her a few rungs on the social mobility ladder. "I put on a suit, and everyone thought I was a college student," Mathison, who is white, said.

Mathison dropped out of high school at 15, and later entered the real estate business. Years of relocating Microsoft and Amazon employees to Seattle homes left Mathison with the means to pursue a degree at the University of Washington School of Medicine. But the opportunities have also left her with a gnawing obligation to the region's original inhabitants.

"The history of our country is extremely unjust. A lot of white people think we're off the hook because it wasn't our choice," she said.

White settlers and soldiers were already flowing into Washington before the 1855 Treaty of Point Elliott was signed. The agreement guaranteed fishing and hunting rights on "usual and accustomed grounds" for the signatory tribes, and reservations were established for the Suquamish, Swinomish, Lummi, and Tulalip people. In exchange, the U.S. gained legal title to land from Mount Rainier—known to Coast Salish tribes as Tahoma—to the Canada border 150 miles to the north, and from the Cascades to the Salish Sea. Today, that sprawling area incorporates the Seattle metro area. More than 4 million people and some of the world's most valuable companies inhabit the space.

Point Elliott was one of about 370 treaties entered into by the United States and Native tribes between 1778 and 1871. Like the others, this one was quickly violated by the U.S. Among other indignities, tribes involved in Point Elliott and other Washington treaties were denied their hunting and fishing rights for more than a century.

But it wasn't just the federal and state governments pressing Indian residents. In 1865, the Seattle Board of Trustees passed Ordinance No. 5, which banished Natives from the town. The ordinance lasted just two years, but was one component of irreparable damage during the era. Construction of the Northern Pacific Railroad and a ship canal connecting Lake Washington and the Puget Sound dried up the wetlands near Native villages or demolished them outright; the rest were set ablaze.

By 1910, as the city of Seattle experienced a surge in population to 237,000 and booming economy reminiscent of its modern day, a Bureau of Indian Affairs agent estimated 1,000 to 3,000 Native Americans experienced homelessness in their homeland. Some starved to death during the winters.

"There's so much history that I wasn't taught," said Mathison. Further enlightened, the lifelong Seattleite decided to start giving monthly contributions to Real Rent Duwamish in November 2019. The program, organized by the Coalition of Anti-Racist Whites in Seattle, supports educational initiatives and maintenance at the Duwamish Longhouse and Cultural Center in southwest Seattle. To date, more than 30,000 people have made a contribution.

"What's happening is a social justice movement, not a monetary issue," said Jolene Haas, the director of the Duwamish Longhouse.

The Real Rent Duwamish initiative is similar to one adopted near San Francisco, where residents can pay a "Shuumi land tax" to the Sogorea Te' Land Trust, an intertribal group trying to return Bay Area land to Native stewardship. Five hours up the coast, in Humboldt Bay, residents can make a voluntary payment to the Wiyot Nation.

Washington state has 29 federally recognized tribes, but the Duwamish is not among them. Many people of Duwamish descent ended up living in the nearby Suquamish, Muckleshoot, and Tulalip reservations, but about 600 others maintain affiliation with the separate Duwamish entity. A lack of federal recognition means the tribe lacks reservation land, nor are its members eligible for assistance from the federal government. Members are supported instead by the nonprofit Duwamish Tribal Services. "Because we don't get federal funds, a lot of our people are forced to go to reservations if they can show ancestry," Haas said.

A four-decade push for federal recognition came to fruition in 2001, it seemed, when the Clinton administration signed off. But the Bush administration reversed the decision, and Duwamish recognition was again denied in 2015. An appeal is pending with the Interior Department. "We may not have recognition or our land," said Chairwoman Cecile Hansen. "But we still have the First Amendment right to speak and not be silenced."

The Duwamish's predicament with federal recognition highlights just how complicated the idea of universal restitution for the Native population is. Unlike possible reparations for descendents of enslaved Africans, restitution for the Indigenous community would most likely rest on tribal affiliation rather than race or ethnicity. The scheme, and the colonialism it hatched from, lays the cobblestones for intra-community squabbling, and according to Haas.

"White supremacy and the government has set us up to fight each other over issues of sovereignty," she said. "Recognition [from the government] wouldn't be necessary if not for this divide and conquer strategy."

Indeed, not all in the Indigenous community are aligned with her tribe's quest to gain recognition, nor with those offering up financial assistance.

"Help isn't paying rent to a non-federally recognized tribe living in the city limits," said Stevenson, the Muckleshoot council member. "It's reaching out to the federally recognized tribes attempting to improve the health of this region."

The Muckleshoot, a tribal nation of people of Duwamish and Upper Puyallup descent whose reservation sits south of Seattle, has long opposed the recognition bid of the Duwamish. The situation is a delicate one both for the local Native community and for non-Natives who want to support Indigenous communities without causing further divisiveness.

For Mathison's part, she feels that paying rent to the Duwamish is a starting point. "Now we are not off the hook, because knowing how unequal history has disproportionately benefited white Americans, we are offered a choice to repay some of that inequality," she said.

Stevenson believes the appropriate starting point in any discussion of reparations is for Seattle residents of all races to inform themselves of tribal history.

"How many of Seattle's new tech workers know about the first peoples of this land? The only way we can grow from our history and trauma is through communication, education and collaboration," he said. It's why he has mixed feelings about the land acknowledgements done at non-Native gatherings. These often occur in the form of signs (on a Seattle church: "We ... acknowledge that we are on the unceded ancestral lands of the Duwamish people ...") or public proclamations before events.

"There's a degree of power we find in public acknowledgements, and that can be profound. But they're also often historical," said Stevenson. And it's that focus on what was, as opposed to what is, that bothers him. "Most [recognition] is very stereotypical. It's about the 'wise savage,' the 'beautiful princess,' but not the exploration of three-dimensional human beings."

Nor do land acknowledgments usually address the systemic hardships and discrimination faced by the Indigenous community. "That history is part of my everyday identity," said Stevenson. "It created so much multigenerational trauma. That's the sad and painful truth about our people today. We're overrepresented in social categories you don't want to be present in, and underrepresented in ones you do."

The overrepresented categories? Short life expectancy (5.5 years less than Americans of all other races), poverty rate (one in four), and those experiencing homelessness (highest rate in the city of Seattle).

To Stevenson, remedial education about local tribes is essential to any form of restitution. One such example is coming to the city's professional football stadium. Beginning next year, Seahawks fans flooding into CenturyLink Field's northern entrance will find themselves in Muckleshoot Plaza, which will showcase a historical narrative of the tribe. The partnership came about after the Seahawks reached out to the Muckleshoot about honoring the tribe's identity in a visible way. The Muckleshoot have struck up a similar partnership with Seattle's soon-to-be National Hockey League team.

Just one generation ago, Stevenson points out, his father, who was adopted by a white family, couldn't technically live in Seattle's Normandy Park neighborhood due to racially restrictive housing covenants. So a partnership with the city's professional sports teams is an improvement, but still not enough.

He gleans hope from Native leaders carrying on the tradition of the successful Indian Rights movement in the Northwest. Beginning in the 1950s, Native leaders like Billy Frank Jr., Nisqually, and Puyallup tribal member Robert Satiacum were instrumental in re-establishing tribal fishing rights and instigated the famous Boldt Decision in 1974, which ruled that Washington's tribes had treaty rights to fish in off-reservation waters, and to 50 percent of the state's annual commercial catch.

"We stand on the shoulders of the leaders who came before, who have called on Seattle to be the city it aspires to be. Our children are watching us. We borrow the earth from them," Stevenson said. It's measures like the Seahawks partnership, he said, that can start to hammer home an important lesson: "This city doesn't exist without our people."

The obsidian scrawl was straightforward: *By the mid 1860s, as the Seattle area was being settled, these people had been assimilated ...*

To Seattle City Councilmember Debora Juarez, the sign in Seattle's Thornton Creek Park was akin to a Confederate monument standing in an African American neighborhood.

"This is just wrong. These people are still here," said Juarez, a member of the Blackfeet tribe and the city's first enrolled Native American councilmember. The Seattle Parks Department removed the sign last year. Now it hangs in Juarez's City Hall office, an artifact of the fiction she's helping to dismantle.

With assistance from Seattle's Native community, the removal of this sign and similar ones in the coming months is a step—albeit a small one, she said—toward grappling with Seattle's history. Juarez hopes to replace the signs with more accurate narratives, and the city has hired Native artists to create iconography celebrating its Indigenous residents.

"It's decolonizing and deconstructing some of the symbols that are not actually Salish symbols. And working with Indigenous people to say that when you land in the city of Seattle, you should be able to look around and say: 'This is Salish People,'" Juarez said in January, two days after being sworn in for her second term.

During the swearing-in ceremony, she ceded much of her time to Suquamish Chairman Leonard Forsman. The scene—a Native woman, elected to a civic body once openly hostile to the Suquamish people, stepping aside for its modern leader to speak—was deliberate.

"Our people died for you and I to sit here, to have a house, to vote, to be called a human being. There's a real beauty in a strange, raw way," said Juarez, who previously led Washington's Office of Indian Affairs. "Just think how amazing we are, that we are still here."

This idea animates Juarez's city council work. She has helped pass resolutions that oppose a liquified natural gas facility in nearby Tacoma and take action to curb the number of missing and murdered Indigenous women in the city.

But Juarez faces one challenge common to people of color in positions of authority. Call it the Obama syndrome—the pressure to represent the thoughts, yearnings, and talking points of an entire race or community. That complexity bore out in 2017, when the city divested from Wells Fargo because it financed the Dakota Access Pipeline.

Juarez started fielding calls from tribal leaders; one contingent was ecstatic about the action, but another took umbrage as the bank financed many of the tribe's vital services.

"I had to hear both sides," she said. Seattle's Native community, after all, is no monolith.

The 36,000 or so Native people who live in the Seattle metro area hail from tribes near and far. "Seattle has a ways to go, but it's ahead of the curve in many ways," said Russell Brooks, a Southern Cheyenne tribal member who moved to Seattle in 2011 from Montana. The filmmaker is now executive director of Red Eagle Soaring, a theatre serving Native youth in the area.

He points to the city, at least superficially, celebrating Native culture with the National Football League's Seahawks team insignia, and the increasingly common land acknowledgements. But there is more tangible action. Seattle opened a tiny-home village for Native people experiencing homelessness last fall. In 2015, the state legislature mandated that tribal sovereignty lessons be included in the public education curriculum—a measure that Red Eagle Soaring supported. "You want the greater public to have a basic level of competency when it comes to tribes and their cultural status," Brooks said. "You want Native students to be able to go to school and not be teased for having braids."

For Heaton, the Indigenous rights activist, reparation actions must graduate from voluntary to systemic. "Monthly giving is nice, but it's the same as if you stop using plastic straws to save the environment," she said. A good place to start, in her mind, is to stop supporting oil and gas activity that isn't welcome in Indian Country; she advocated for Seattle's City Council to divest its financial holdings from Wells Fargo (In 2018, the city resumed banking with Wells

Fargo after finding no alternatives). To that end, she co-founded Mazaska Talks, an organization that aims to help individuals compel cities and banks to divest from polluting industries.

Fern Renville, a member of the Sisseton Wahpeton Oyate, moved to Seattle in the 1980s. She teaches about Coast Salish culture in Puget Sound elementary schools, and believes the Pacific Northwest can serve as a model not only for restitution, but for how Indigenous leadership can spark societal advancement. Youth, she said, can look to the examples of Frank and Satiacum, the fishing-rights protesters, as well as a growing contingent of modern leaders.

"Our water is cleaner than it used to be because local tribes fought for it. The tribes here have fought and won to take down dams to save the orca and salmon. And the governor appointed the first Native American judge [Raquel Montoya-Lewis] in Washington's history," she said.

Renville's perspective as a member of a plains tribe living in the Northwest gives her a nuanced viewpoint on reparations. She brought up the 1980 Supreme Court case, *United States v. Sioux Nation of Indians*, in which the government was ordered to pony up $17 million for taking the Black Hills of South Dakota in violation of the 1868 Treaty of Fort Laramie. To this day, the Great Sioux Nation has not accepted the money; doing so, its leaders have argued, would constitute the willing sale of something that was stolen. The account, held in trust, now holds more than $1 billion.

To some, a payout of that size would be a form of reparations. But Renville said repairing historical wrongdoings in Indian Country is far more complicated than cash. Any approach to tribal reparations would have to be done on a tribe-by-tribe basis, and in a different way than reparations have been discussed for other racial groups.

"I understand the economic viewpoint because of the labor aspect for African Americans," she said. "I'm not averse to receiving financial reparations personally, but I know very few tribal citizens comfortable with it."

Reparations are often framed as something given from transgressors to those aggrieved. *Sorry for taking the Black Hills; here's $1 billion.* But to many Native Americans who spoke for this story, reparation isn't something white Americans should bestow upon them. Rather, it's returning to a leadership position in land that was always theirs.

"We should really stop with the white saviorism when it comes to Native issues and this country," Renville said. "These problems are interconnected, and white leadership isn't entitled to solve them as only they see fit."

In her City Hall office, Juarez pointed to a photo of Shirley Chisholm. "For so long, the Native community looked at the African American community for our heroes," she said, but a sea change may be afoot. Deb Haaland of New Mexico and Sharice Davids of Kansas became the first Native American women elected to Congress in 2018. Locally, Juarez said Indigenous rights advocates and sisters Colleen Echohawk and Abigail Echo-Hawk (they spell their last names differently), who have been instrumental in addressing Native homelessness and the violence against Native women, are figures the Seattle community can look up to. Maybe it's their very presence, shaping policy at levels from the municipal to the federal, that will build momentum toward restitution 160 years in the making.

After all, every leader, every land acknowledgement, every uncomfortable conversation, every teachable moment can make a difference, said Brooks. Despite the complexity and magnitude of a topic like reparations for Native Americans, he believes there is actually a very simple question at the heart of it.

"We are all Indigenous to this earth," he said. "Reparations isn't about a guilt trip. It's saying, 'We're here now, we may have all been colonized at one point, but how do we live neighborly?'"

A Troubled Childhood Should Not Be a Precursor to a Life of Crime

I knew him as William.

To much of the city and the gymgoers at my neighborhood Planet Fitness who saw his lean, angular face consume the pixels of the overhead TV monitors, he was just another alleged criminal.

That much was assured after 24-year-old William Tolliver and his friend, Marquise Tolbert, allegedly ignited a shootout in downtown Seattle two weeks ago that killed a woman and wounded seven others, including a 9-year-old boy. (After being arrested in Las Vegas, both William and Marquise face charges of first-degree murder and six counts of assault in the first degree.)

Your heart breaks for the eight people and their families whose lives will never be the same. It shatters when you know the person who helped cause their pain.

William is a cousin of my youngest brother, whom my parents adopted when I was in high school.

I hadn't seen William since he was a teenager, over five years ago. His visits to my parents' home in those early days were marked by a foreboding sadness. My immediate family worried about him, a fear borne of William's constant exposure to drugs, gangs, violence, and petty robberies. As a teenager from a troubled home, he seemed at times to be raising himself.

The scant invocations he heard of the consequences of his chosen path were no match for the bludgeoning by his chaotic environment.

Violent situations spawn violent people. It doesn't matter if you have a two-parent household if neither parent supports positive life choices. It becomes a cycle that, unless disrupted, continues indefinitely.

It's why it's so hard for me to sympathize with the clamor of voices demanding more policing in response to the downtown violence. Seattle Mayor Jenny Durkan, noting the hiring effort underway by the Seattle Police Department, told KOMO News, "We want more police officers." A sheriff's deputy, speaking anonymously to conservative commentator Jason Rantz, advocated harsher tactics and cited New York City's discredited and racist "stop and frisk" policy as a proven method for cleaning up the streets. A growing chorus of social media posts have also pleaded for more punitive responses to drug crimes.

I understand the knee jerk fear triggered by the violence in downtown Seattle. But to witness William's life trajectory from an impressionable boy to a steel-hearted young man is to recognize the futility of draconian responses to crime.

Solutions to our city's recent tragedies cannot be driven by fear, or else we risk unleashing further trauma upon youth and already traumatized communities. This is the assessment of many community leaders I spoke with who stress the importance of strategic mentorship over aggressive policing.

Proven crime-prevention strategies

"Being reactive is only a bandage in these situations," says Marty Jackson, the southeast network executive director of the Boys and Girls Club of King County. "We have to remind folks of the unintended consequences of policy fueled by fear and false narratives. There's a lot of historic trauma and harm by law enforcement."

Jackson has mentored hundreds of South Seattle kids over two decades, and says she's had several emotional conversations with youth since the Jan. 22 shooting. Most have revolved around their concerns that the dominant cultural narrative around violence prevention isn't fully informed by what's working. And, according to Jackson, what's working has been both mentoring and community-led programs aimed at supporting teenagers.

She points to the current Rainier Beach: A Beautiful Safe Place for Youth Initiative. The place-based violence prevention initiative, initially funded by a grant from the Department of Justice before the city took over funding in 2016, decreased youth violence in five crime "hot spots" around the South Seattle neighborhood between 2011 and 2018.

The violence prevention initiative relied on five non-arrest strategies, including "corner greeter" stations, where youth offered passersby refreshments; a "safe passage" program in which adults escorted youth leaving school; and relationship building between businesses and youth. The results showed a decline in violent crime (assaults, armed robbery), particularly youth crime, in the five designated hotspots compared with the rest of the South Precinct.

Research assessing the initiative showed that crackdowns and arrests were effective at reducing crime in a specific hotspot. But the true impact of those actions is less clear. Arrests and prosecution actually increased the likelihood that those caught would reoffend elsewhere.

Early contact with the justice system puts kids on a path toward violent and chronic offending as adults, according to a study published in the Western Criminology Review. With 44 arrests on his record before Las Vegas police apprehended William, his life provides tragic confirmation of the data.

It's why Jackson says the city can't afford to make "emotionally charged" decisions when it comes to public policy and should commit to looking closely at proven strategies for preventing violence.

"I'm not at all trying to trivialize the shootings that happened. I want to feel safe, too, the same as everyone else," says Jackson.

"We have to understand that these young men are also part of our community, through the good and bad."

'WE'VE BEEN WALKING THIS PATH FOR DECADES'

The adage that "hurt people hurt people" is one retired King County Superior Court Judge Wesley Saint Clair knows well. He came face to face with thousands of young people who filtered through the juvenile court he presided over for nearly 16 years.

"I remember listening to two boys who were first robbed by fists, then by gunpoint, then three years later started robbing people themselves," he says. "Our systemic response isn't, how do we heal children—who've been hurt—in healthy ways? And because of that, [those children] end up asking, 'How can I inflict this pain on someone else?' "

Saint Clair says the vast majority of the youth who came through his courtroom, even those charged with murder, were anguished by their decisions and were still maturing.

"Their brains weren't mature, and don't do so until they turn 25," he says, referring to the current neuroscience on brain development.

Over the years, it became undeniable that those summoned to his courtroom were in need of love.

"Young people want boundaries. They want to be guided along a path of some sorts. They want you to grieve with them when they're struggling, and to validate them and listen to them," he says.

That shouldn't mean we dismiss a young person's agency in their decision making, but we should also examine our society's own agency in contributing to their plight.

A recent visit to Monroe Prison illuminated the point for Saint Clair. Of the prisoners he spoke with—some he'd crossed paths with as a judge—most had never had a sustained positive influence in their lives. Statistics show that one-time wards of the state are almost 66% more likely to end up in jail, a clarion sign that we are failing to take care of children at the most vulnerable and formative years of their lives.

Saint Clair says society needs to be more proactive. That means applying preventive methods from an early age and identifying behavioral patterns that can signal red flags at home, including inappropriate language and violent hitting as early as first and second grade. This awareness needs to be paired with peer-to-peer mentors—that is, case workers with a similar lived experience—who can be responsive to the complex needs of our youth. And there needs to be a long-lasting commitment, at least 10 to 15 years, suggests Saint Clair.

"We've been walking this path for decades," says Saint Clair. "It's going to take decades to get us out of it."

There isn't a jail sentence long enough to replace a caring adult. There isn't a jail large enough to deter the seeking of belonging that gangs many times provide. There isn't enough fear that will ever replace the words "I love you," and "you matter to me."

This was continually reinforced to me over the past 10 years I have served as a youth mentor. It requires heaps of patience, endurance and resolve. But so do most things worth doing.

Right after the holidays, the weather caromed from rain to sunshine in that signature Seattle way. I was at work in the library when I bumped into Noah, an old mentee of mine from the Youth Tutoring Program.

Now a student at Whatcom Community College, he used to carry around a heavy indifference to school and most everything else.

As we chatted, I remembered all the days I wanted to stop showing up to our sessions at the Lake Washington Tutoring Center. I kept telling myself, "This is too hard. I'm wasting my time. Nothing's sinking in. ..."

In that moment with Noah, I felt so glad I kept going. We embraced before saying goodbye.

He walked out the doors. The rain had cleared. Nothing but sunlight before him.

Our World Needs More Truth, Fewer Saviors

GRADUATES, I WISH I COULD TELL YOU to count yourselves lucky today.

However, I can't pretend the future is imminently bright and this world will default to justice and peace as long as you work hard, hope, and align with our society's current notions of progress.

Over the last few months, those dictums have been revealed for the fables they are, unconcealing, for some of you, a world teetering on the knife's edge of despair.

But though we currently find ourselves shackled to a rollercoaster of uncertainty, we can still force a brief halt to pause and reflect on attainments both realized and desired.

You've just spent years, whether through intention or inertia, dedicated to becoming something other than what you were. Changing, growing, and evolving right along with our world, all while attempting to find a place for yourself in it. You've exhibited an impressive amount of discipline and creativity by designing your own academic path, especially in times like these.

And I'm sure I don't have to tell you in this day and age, or any day and age, how hard trying to change this world is.

Much harder, though, is attempting that feat without losing the vessel you'll need to change it: namely, yourself.

That's why today, future leaders, when you're expecting a series of platitudes demanding you seize the day, reach for the sky, realize the impossible dream, and all the other cliches you'll be bazooka-blasted with upon opening your congratulatory graduation cards, I have none.

Instead, I offer truth. And though truth owes us no solace, it can sometimes prompt change. And if this last decade in movement and social justice journalism has taught me anything, it's that radical self-honesty is the best source of fuel for the work we must do to help shift this planet's fortunes.

Like many of you reading this, I had a thirst for leaving the world a better place than the one I was born into.

Other than personal torment thanks to an internal war between doing the right thing and the most lucrative, that was the reason I abandoned the world I'd joined after college—one of moneymaking for the filthy rich and their grossly inflated salaries—to barter my soul back and embark on a career in journalism. I was inspired by Plato's axiom that storytellers rule the world, so they are best positioned to change it.

What most needed changing at the time were perceptions about the part of the city I grew up in: South Seattle.

It was at one time the most diverse zip code in the United States, with over 57 ethnicities and 88 languages spoken. It was also one of the poorest areas in this big, rich town. Media coverage other than crime and high school basketball was non-existent.

Cutting my teeth at a small paper, one of my first assignments was asking residents of South Seattle to share positive experiences about their home. I ended up speaking to a young man who had barely scratched 19. I asked him to highlight what he felt was good about our community.

"Nothing," he said, dryly. "Nothing at all."

Eventually, I asked him why he felt that way. He said it was because "they never say anything good about us. We're always drug dealers. We're always gangbangers. Our lives don't matter." He was talking about the media.

Emphasizing pain and tragedy, those stories had come to define his community. I told him that I was here to tell a different one. He said he "hoped so," but he couldn't see it happening.

We parted ways, and I never saw him again, because a little over two weeks later, he was found about a mile away from where we met, dead with a gun in his hand and a bullet in his chest. I still don't know why, or what he died for, other than it all being senseless and avoidable.

I frequently wish I would've said something more to him. I thought maybe if he had something to change his mind about himself and his home, maybe it could've changed his destiny.

That something became the *South Seattle Emerald*, this six-year-old publication which continues to magnify its community's nuances, intricacies, and gradations.

The mantra of journalism has long been that it exists to speak truth to power. And as much as I bought into that then, and still do, I thought its superior purpose was speaking truth to those who believe they are powerless and reminding them that they are not.

And so for the next six years, we hoped to tell a different story in South Seattle and POC communities that might not only change hearts and minds, but policies and lives.

We hoped to demolish every -ism and social phobia from ableism to racism to sexism, from anti-semitism to transphobia and homophobia. And we'd do it by showing how these fears and bigotries seeped into and operated within the everyday structures of society.

Starting with nothing but dwindling savings and a room in my parents' home, we fought to do just that through grueling 20-hour workdays, seven days a week—barely surviving off $500 in a "good" month. Those jokes about being 30-something and living in your mother's basement became a lot less funny because that was my life.

It was a life of perpetual sacrifices for others not named Marcus. One of perpetual fighting as a champion for those who couldn't or wouldn't speak up for themselves because society had muffled them. One of perpetual neglect of a life outside of my social justice work.

I found myself fortunate enough to be immersed in the company of changemakers, thought leaders, and social justice warriors (I don't use that phrase pejoratively) who could inject bursts of hope and inspiration into crowds and influence policymakers.

I just as often encountered people with eyes locked on a better world, but who had lost sight of themselves as human beings, pressured to live up to some hero status, glorified beyond reality.

There were many—too many—civic and community leaders who experienced a planet-sized void in their lives. When you stripped away their function, their title, and their reputation, there was nothing left for them to identify themselves. Nearly dehumanized by playing the role of local messiahs, they couldn't assess their own worth. It's what happens when you give yourself away and keep giving until there's nothing left for you.

This isn't only second-hand knowledge I'm sharing, though. This is also a personal experience. Because after years of running on fumes just to keep pace with the work of bringing light to the world, I ended up at the darkest point of my life.

It was the result of having no breathing room between my aspirations and my identity. I leaned heavily on alcohol, abusing it and other drugs, and became suicidal at one point, all in an attempt to flee from a bipolar diagnosis. The idea of failing to live up to what others expected of me filled my mind with terror.

I'm now nearly two years into recovery from alcoholism and am steadily rebuilding my life from that attempt to end it. I've realized how little regard I'd given to the voice inside of me telling me that self-nourishment was not selfishness and that part of believing in a better world is actually taking time to enjoy, reflect, and pay witness to how you choose to live in the one we have.

Underneath its unrelenting frenzy, the world offers stillness. That stillness can be used to probe deeply into undiscovered regions of ourselves. And what you'll most likely uncover is what I did: not a savior placed on some pedestal surrounded by unattainable expectations, but someone this world is more desperately in need of: you, along with your awareness, your foundational values, and your capacity to do all you can do for the betterment of our society—but not more.

You'll find someone who should never be elevated to perfection because of your work, nor down to inadequacy because of your flaws. You have to exist in the space between the two—fully human, faltering, committing errors, and owning your mistakes. Purpose can be an enhancement, but never a substitute for self-worth.

So, in all your pursuits, don't build up others at the cost of destroying yourself. Don't seek societal salvation through the tool of self-destruction. Harder than individual sacrifice is a duty-bound commitment to the arduous process of societal improvement, forged from shared visions, possibilities, and responsibilities for one another as well as yourself. Such a vow replaces self-worship with self and social assessment.

Refrain from grand declarations of wokeness for all the world to see; go about the day-to-day business of chipping away at them without acclaim. That is durable. That is replicable. It's also essential to steer this swiveling marble away from its current course.

This world, as you know, is in critical need of an altered path. It's crying out for a new way of imagining life.

This world is not yet just when it has more black people locked in jail now than were slaves before Emancipation. This world is not yet fair when 26 people possess more wealth than half of the world's population. This world is not yet compassionate when we continue to poison our oceans and our air, leaving future generations to suffer the consequences. No, this world is constantly engaged in acts of hate, in the exploitation of marginalized classes and the oppression of the vulnerable by fraudulent authorities—always claiming superiority above, not similarity alongside them.

I'm certain that comes as no shock to you.

And nor will my next refrain, but it bears repeating. It's something I wish I would've told myself after meeting that young man who died senselessly all those years ago. It's something I wish I would've told myself every single day I lived.

This world needs you. And I do mean it needs *you*.

It needs you with all your blemishes. It needs you to be courageous when you're faced with fear. It needs you to be humble when you're called on your behavior. It needs you to collaborate when you want to forge ahead alone because you think you know better than the people you're trying to help.

It needs you to seek change, not as a proxy for your authentic identity, but as an obligation of service to those who came before you and will continue living after you. It needs you to rest, recharge, and renew yourself, knowing there are others doing this work, too. It needs you to seek knowledge of what you don't understand and for you to know that you will never outpace the work needed to be more loving, more accepting, and more empathic. It needs you to be fully human: never perfect, yet improving.

And so, today, Class of 2020, I have no luck to offer or hope to give. Instead, I have much to ask of you in the days ahead.

I ask you to seek community when you feel isolated in your endeavors. I ask that you cultivate resilience for times when your character will be tried by circumstance. I ask that you embrace complexity over simplification, because this world is spectacularly complicated. I ask that you interrogate the beliefs you hold about yourself and others when those beliefs are justifiably challenged. I ask you to anguish as mightily over society's misdeeds as you do over a sole individual's failings. I ask that you question a society where murder and discrimination are illegal and yet people continue to murder and discriminate without consequence.

I ask that you examine any system of authority devaluing the many for the enrichment of the few and that you ask not for an apology for its existence, but a wholesale transformation of its enterprise.

I ask, in this interconnected web of humanity, that you never allow one strand to dominate the others, so as to avoid our inevitable unraveling. I ask that you find your truth in life, impervious to bombast and enmity and that you stand in it unshakably.

And I ask that you continue to know, love, accept, and learn about yourself, just as much as you do this ever-shifting world. I ask that right now when you face a time like none before, you find fertile minds where understanding, openness, and human reciprocity are blossoming like never before—and that you join them. And though it will take time, with an arrival date different for everyone, I ask that you someday find yourself, as I do today, equipped to endure all that life has in store for you.

May your answers change our world.

Congratulations, Class of 2020, on this day and all the days you'll live.

I Glimpsed Hope in a South Seattle Park

Breonna Taylor, Tamir Rice, Sandra Bland. It had been another string of ungodly killings of Black Americans. I was tired of exterminated Black life. My soul had grown increasingly weary from false hopes, empty promises and muscular words that atrophy by inaction.

I swore off Black Lives Matter marches and rallies. They were placebos unable to quell intensifying pain.

The last one I attended occurred after the killings of Philando Castile and Alton Sterling by police officers in 2016. Submerged in tormented shouts of "Black Lives Matter," I situated myself in downtown's Westlake Park where the march began. My cynicism anchored me there, kept me from proceeding, while the mass of people and their chanting moved farther up Pine Street.

Nailing me in place was the conviction that this country would never care for Black people. At least never care more than enough to believe that uttering the right phrase would absolve oneself of racism. It would only ever subordinate Black Americans' unique struggles as identity politics, never critical priorities. It would never stop believing that one exceptional individual with black skin placed in a position of power somehow meant racial equality, or that racism was over. It would continue to believe in the magical thinking that says racial justice is achieved by class equality.

Any visions I possessed of a better world perished as the deaths of Black people mounted. I resigned myself to the belief that I'd never witness a nonracist world in my lifetime, or any other. I thought time devoted to marches and rallies raging against Black death was better spent alongside my family. There was no telling when others might be chanting their name. A police encounter could sweep them to the grave in an instant, as it had with Garner and Taylor and all the others. So I needed to cherish them now, as often and as deeply as I could.

In my brother Antonio, I saw a man who has grown from his insecurities as an adoptee to a firm but fair basketball coach, now inspiring youth in the south end, a man who I can debate endlessly, and comically, about who is actually the greatest basketball player of all time (obviously it's Lebron). Once a boy who blazed with anger over his life's circumstances, he had become a man whose jokes make our family laugh so hard that BBQ sauce flies from our mouths at family barbecues.

In him, I saw what society wouldn't. It would see his skin and broad stature as a fear multiplier.

How, in a society where police kill Black people at a rate 2.5 times higher than whites, would he not one day be reduced to a threat? Or killed jogging, the same way as Ahmaud Arbery was?

In my precious, 18-month-old great-niece Sierra, with her french fry obsession and chubby cheeks, I saw unbridled joy. But I knew society could one day condemn her to the ranks of the 39% of Black children who live in poverty or the 27.4% of Black Americans who live in poverty as adults. How would society not prematurely end her life with a no-knock warrant turned fatal, as it has for at least three Black women since 2003?

No, I thought back then, better to spend as much time as I could while they were here.

This was the despondency and resignation I felt as the fires started to blaze in Minneapolis late last month. I had little hope these embers would spark a revolution. I felt this even as marches proliferated in small towns that heretofore didn't seem to know Black life existed, let alone mattered. But something began to stir inside me last Sunday, as I watched nearly 10,000 demonstrators representing a multiplicity of life pour into the meadow at Othello Park in South Seattle. I began to think not about the dead, but about the living, remembering that I was part of the latter, and what being a member of its ranks means for our future.

On a day usually reserved for worship of the Christian faith, I found my own belief restored in humanity.

Derrick Wheeler-Smith, one of the organizers of last Sunday's "We Want to Live" rally, was as good a proselytizer as any. Skeptical of how mainstream media might cover a Black Lives Matter protest hosted in South Seattle, he asked that I attend so I could see the truth for myself.

With the Seattle Police Department largely absent, in compliance with the wishes of organizers, he wanted me to experience the momentum that had accrued after 10 days of protests, the masses of everyday people across class, race and gender, all motivated by the desire for a society without racism.

As the sun shined down that afternoon, I stood in Othello Park, awash in a sea of rallygoers in black shirts and medical masks, a crowd larger than any I've ever seen in over 30 years of visiting that park. The calls of Black

Lives Matter were familiar. The sight of allies of all races, with signs that read "White Silence is Violence" and "Not again," was, too.

In the middle of a rapturous affirmation of Black lives, I wondered if the aftermath of this moment would be any different from all the other ripples that had dissolved instead of cresting into society-shaping waves?

And so I asked people the only question I felt mattered on this day. How do we sustain this latest collective awakening?

I admire the formal organizations that are carrying the load of this movement both nationally and locally. But it is everyday people who form the heartbeat of a culture that pumps blood into our politics, our culture and our civic life. Until they change drastically, nothing else will.

Recent developments had begun to soften my cynicism. The *New York Times* bestseller list turning into an anti-racist reading guide; Dallas adopting a "duty to intervene" rule requiring officers to stop other cops who are engaging in inappropriate use of force; more Confederate monuments being removed in Southern states; a sitting Washington state Senator expressing a commitment to fight racism in ourselves and our communities on the Senate floor—all this slowly began to persuade me that something was changing.

But more than anything, I have been moved seeing previously "colorblind" neighbors and roommates replacing escapist entertainment on their YouTube feeds with daily video lectures dissecting how structural racism works and manifests itself in society. A subject that once provoked indifference now captured their full concentration.

That quiet consistency, while perhaps not as dramatic as marching, can be just as profound, and just as necessary, according to Lindsay Hill, a veteran of all those marches I'd been absent from the last five years. She sees something now that has been missing from them in the past.

"For the first time, I feel like people do see the personal impact [of racism]," says Hill. But she had been cautious of getting her hopes up that change would follow George Floyd's death, as she had witnessed so little after those of Eric Garner, Tamir Rice and Trayvon Martin.

Hill visited Ferguson, Missouri, last year on the anniversary of Michael Brown's death. She says the feeling is palpably different this time, possibly due in part to the coronavirus pandemic raging through the country, causing people to understand how much one person's humanity depends on the health and safety of others.

Of course, it's hard not to acknowledge the possibility that this is an instance of "fool me once, shame on you, fool me twice, shame on me," as Hill put it. But, she added, she thinks she's "sold" on people being committed to the journey this time. I, too, believe there are more fellow travelers than before.

Hill also noted that after the massacre of nine Black parishioners in Charleston, South Carolina, there were relatively few companies who put out statements. In the wake of George Floyd's killing, it's easier to count the organizations who didn't, with even the National Football League issuing a mea culpa for ignoring its players on matters of racial justice.

But for Hill, ordinary people are the ultimate forecasters of our future, and their recent actions give reason for hope that the clouds of chaos will abate. Coming from a Friday march, she and her family passed by Columbia City homes in a neighborhood that was once predominately Black, but has more recently been referred to as "Mayberry" by *The Seattle Times*. She saw the white homeowners outside their homes holding up Black Lives Matter signs, with other almost exclusively white people honking in support of a message that should become a social maxim.

"Our humanity is intertwined," she says. "We are all not OK until every one of us is. I just started crying as we were driving around."

Soon after, demonstrators formed a massive human amoeba of black, worn in solidarity with the BLM movement, marching 2 miles to the Rainier Beach Safeway. The ending point was deliberate. Just two weeks prior, a young Black man had been shot and killed there.

Organizers overran grounds where death recently commiserated, with a living affirmation of Black life. They brought along a message that requires perpetual resurrection: we always have a choice of hope or despair. Sunday made me choose the former for the first time in nearly half a decade.

Our world remains as it is only by our captivity to the status quo. It is an oppression enforced by our inability to dream of spring in the depths of our society's winters. To know freedom, to know hope, is to allow ourselves the rendering of a world not yet born, but laboring it to be — conversation by conversation, march by march, epiphany by epiphany, day by day.

I see it now. I glimpsed a piece of it last Sunday in Othello Park. This promised land that loves my brother and bubble-cheeked great-niece as much as I do.

How Can We Heal? Braver Angels Test the Notion of Healing Across Political Divides

So many days I wake up without hope for this country.

As I watched the results of our presidential election, the mere fact that nearly half of Americans saw, heard, and knew everything I did about our current president and voted for him anyway affirmed my worst perceptions of this nation.

These months since the pandemic have been a rolling exhibition of American agony. Amid affirmations of Black life ringing from sea to sea, Black people were still terrorized. Our barbarism toward each other continued, as drivers purposely crashed their cars into crowds of peaceful protesters. Lifesaving science remained politicized rather than adopted, and radical extremism—including white supremacist terrorism—festered.

Little is new, but it still terrifies me.

We have monumental problems that must be addressed if we are to function, let alone survive as a society. And yet, it seems no "we" exists to combat our challenges.

Fearful of each other, Americans from all persuasions are stockpiling guns. In our state, September saw an 88%

increase in gun sales versus the same time last year, according to The Trace, a nonprofit media outlet chronicling gun issues.

With our nation's history of terrorizing its marginalized, it's hard to fault the logic of personal armament.

But it's also hard to see how increased hostility ends any other way but terribly for our country.

To be clear, I've always rejected the well-trodden trope rolled out after the 2016 election proselytizing that we "simply need to listen to people" who voted differently than us. That suggests a lopsided relationship, not one where I am heard back, respected, or have my humanity recognized. Marginalized communities have had little choice but to listen throughout American history.

But I also reject the notion that our options are exclusively either absolutist violence or grudging subordination to another's viewpoint.

Seeking an alternative brought me to the Braver Angels Alliance of Seattle-Everett (BAASE), established last November. I'd vaguely remembered the national organization, then known as Better Angels, from a 2018 *New York Times* column. Its website claimed the organization was at the "head of the movement not just to depolarize politics, but to re-imagine what it means to be an American."

I was skeptical.

Initially so was Will Clemmer.

"I was sure it was going to be a shouting match, and an attack on each other's ideas," said Clemmer, now the organization's Washington state coordinator. "When I saw people being able to speak in an environment where people were listening, examining stereotypes, it was like all the pressure went out of the teakettle."

Formed with an equal ratio of those who identified as Red or Blue, the group has hosted workshops, debates, film talks, and book clubs providing civil discourse and a neutral ground for folks of different political persuasions to listen, be heard, be challenged, and reflect. Hopefully over the duration of years, not as one-offs.

"What Braver Angels is doing is helping me [ask] not 'How do I get myself understood better?' but 'How do I understand others better?'" said Mark Church, who identifies as a Blue.

Curiosity from those with opposing viewpoints is what makes Jared Oren, a Red and recent Washington, D.C., transplant, see Braver Angels as a safe haven from being stereotyped.

"No one questions your sincerity here. Whereas, I think in other circles your views automatically are illegitimate, or not worthy of consideration," he said.

Though civil, Braver Angels is not a place where difference is disregarded.

"We actually [get] into that vigorous debate as well, learning from each other and respecting each other's backgrounds," said Christine Cook, a Blue. "And whenever I learn about someone else, actually, I'm learning about myself."

Influenced by family and marriage counseling, Braver Angel debates—including a recent one on the presidential election—don't attempt to change people's minds, or forge more centrists, or vie for ideological supremacy. The goal is to confront difficult issues without unilaterally dismissing those with alternative viewpoints. It recognizes our political decisions have consequences for all of us.

"We say it's being curious instead of furious," said Mary Beth Stibbins, a local chapter founder.

She and other Braver Angels participated in a cross-party prayer vigil (secular and religious) on election night and have adopted the With Malice Toward None pledge, rejecting violence and embracing shared values regardless of the presidential victor.

There is so much praise for a willingness to fight and die for this country, I'm wondering what of the harder things?

How many will practice social humility? How many will recognize that humans are products of our life experiences? How many will pause long enough to recognize the human across our divides, even if we don't relate, agree with, or bear similar pains, even when we've done each other harm? And that unity is not assimilation, but solitary reflection?

I don't know if any of it will work but I'm willing to try.

So, I called a conservative friend I'd stopped speaking with after the 2016 election. He'd been there when I was heartbroken, depressed and broke.

Our politics will never align. But the phone conversation proves our regard for each other always will.

We talked about our families, navigating the pandemic, and our mutual love of the superhero film genre—something I'd forgotten we shared.

Before we hung up, I told him I loved him.

It'd been a long time since we'd heard that from each other.

I Fear Everyday Encounters More Than I Do Hate Groups

HATRED'S BEEN GORGING ON ME for more than a year.

That's around the time I stood amid the sonic boom of voices set off from clashing groups outside the Renton Fairwood library. I was there to cover the controversy surrounding Drag Queen Story Hours, a King County library activity where professional drag queens read LGBTQ-affirming books to children.

Predictably, the event attracted those who viewed it as a Satanic bewitching of children. But it also attracted nearly three times as many who affirmed the story time's inclusionary values. Decibel levels soared as the supportive side roared "love" while the opposition hurled back "shame."

Between them marched children, some as young as 3 and carrying rainbow flags, entering the library to hear drag king Thadayus read *Julián Is a Mermaid*. But they weren't alone. Menacing the proceedings were a group of white supremacists, their faces hidden behind masks, some a hairpin from unhinged, with guns holstered on their side, throwing up the white power symbol to me and a photographer.

Contempt devoured me.

How dare they put toddlers—who'd barely been acquainted with life—at risk should violence break out? I was thankful supporters had largely blocked the white supremacists from the view of the children, but I walked with rage. It's a rage I've carried with me as I've grown increasingly hateful of those who view this nation not as yours or mine, but solely theirs.

It's endured with every news report of an adherent to violent white supremacy who slaughters innocents in El Paso, Texas, assaults rabbis departing their synagogues in San Diego, and absurdly blames Asian Americans for our current pandemic in this woketropolis we call home.

The Department of Homeland Security has billed white supremacy as the "most persistent and lethal threat" currently facing our nation. And although no one gathers locally in meaningful numbers to shriek about being "replaced" by fellow Americans, our city is not free of its own racist pathogens.

As reported last week, Seattle has tracked with national, state and countywide trends showing an increase in hate crimes. The first six months of 2020 saw a 56% increase from the same time period the previous year, according to the Seattle Police Department's online hate crime dashboard.

Unlike FBI hate crime statistics cited for national reporting, Seattle's data includes crimes not motivated by racial bias but containing elements of it, such as someone using a racial slur while committing a robbery. It also counts non-criminal acts like someone using the n-word.

A word apparently streaming from the tongue here.

Every month for the first half of 2020, Blacks were the leading targets of hate crimes. They make up only 7% of our city's population but a third (34%) of hate/bias crimes in the city.

And yet most of the acts aren't conducted by members of the seven Seattle-based hate groups identified by the Southern Poverty Law Center.

Those behaviors are more a product of everyday interactions than bald white supremacy, according to SPD's Bias Crime Coordinator Detective Elizabeth Wareing.

"In the city of Seattle, hate crimes are much closer to home, much more down to earth," said Wareing. "It's someone walking down the street. It's someone in your workplace. Someone where you're out grocery shopping."

That cold splash of water hitting me directly in the face is the reminder that even with a rise in hate crimes and hate groups, the existential threat is the racism in our everyday society, ready to be activated by uncertainty, scapegoating, fear and purposelessness. And that we are all potential victims and perpetrators of it.

Even with Trump gone, we'll do nothing but return to our regularly scheduled racism.

"You cannot get away from it. People just get sucked into the zeitgeist of white supremacy," said Lonnie Lusardo, who conducts diversity and inclusion training as part of the Seattle-based Diversity Collaborative.

Lusardo spent 13 years writing and researching for his book *The Anatomy of Organized Hate*, interviewing dozens of former white extremists to chronicle their journeys in and out of supremacist groups. The book doesn't heroize them for turning their backs on hatred or gloss over their heinous crimes. But it does show the susceptibility of humans to being seduced by a simplistic view of an infinitely complex world.

His work urges a cultural audit forcing us to evaluate those we vote for, who we invite to our dining room tables, and who we include in our social circles. It asks for these assessments from human beings vulnerable to believing we can combat hatred with more of the same. It also provides a warning: we will inevitably become captives of the emotions we repeatedly embrace.

Too irate, I took away the wrong message from that night at the library, when dozens of hatemongers were drowned out by a vast number clearing a pathway to where hate could not enter.

These past four years have seen my hatred unable to overcome its propulsion, rolling over inhumane extremists, Trump supporters, apathetic voters and those clumsily awakening to the realities of racism. But I'm tired of hating. I'm tired of simply seething in a broken world, rather than advancing a better one built on mercy, justice, and compassion.

Aren't you?

How I Survived the Collision of Racism and the Stigma of Mental Illness

Survivor's guilt terrorizes me sometimes. Why am I so lucky when others sharing my complexion and battling mental health struggles are not? That question arises every time I read about Black people with mental illnesses killed by police: Charleena Lyles, Daniel Prude, Manuel Ellis. Their specters summon us to the reality of a nation besotted with violence and indifferent to the vulnerable.

The 55 people with mental illnesses killed in Washington state by police since 2015, according to The Washington Post's police-shooting database, also prompt reflection on my luck in avoiding their fate as I live with bipolar disorder.

In 2018, I had a psychotic episode in the middle of downtown Seattle. Walking down Fifth Avenue, with a mind crammed with carnage, I nearly destroyed my lungs screaming that I wanted to kill myself.

My mother was by my side.

Nearly a foot shorter and 60 pounds lighter, she could only pray. My sizzling brain cells were impervious to pleas of reason.

Frightened for her son, she had only two options: somehow calm me down enough to try to stuff me into an Uber headed for family and friends, or call 911.

She did a rapid assessment: Black man, non-responsive, frantic. She pictured a police encounter quickly escalating into violence.

"What if they kill my son?"

She wanted to avoid the gnawing guilt that plagues Joe Prude, as he told *The New York Times*' Daily podcast, after he called the police to assist his brother Daniel during a mental health crisis. Daniel's encounter with them ended in death, ruled a homicide by complications of asphyxia.

Even if my scenario didn't end as grotesquely, what about arrest? Turning me over to a racist criminal justice system would likely terminate any professional ambitions.

She opted not to call. Instead, she braved the horror-on-wheels that was a 30 minute Uber ride with a bellicose son, and a superhumanly patient driver.

My race meant I was six times more likely to be killed by police than a white person is, according to a Harvard study. An untreated mental illness further boosted the likelihood of death by police, 16 times as much, according to the nonprofit Treatment Advocacy Center.

When the bias of race merges with the stigma of mental illness to collide with law enforcement and criminal justice systems inadequately addressing either, what else can be produced except disaster?

"Race matters and it is true that implicit bias does exist. And then you have an officer and someone in a mental health crisis who are experiencing two different realities," says Nikki Jones, a professor of African American Studies at the University of California, Berkeley, who studies encounters between the public and police.

It's why current conversation around reshaping policing and our criminal justice system must be scrutinized in the context of officers being utilized as intended by society, says Jones.

"Another way we think about policing is as an institution that allows for a sufficient distribution of violence into the public. Violence is a centrality to policing. It's demonstrated in the ability and the effort to defend police to use violence," says Jones.

Of course that violence is not equally distributed in society. Jones points to a recent Pew poll that showed 56% of police officers agreed that it's more useful to be aggressive in "certain" areas of the city.

That's a subtler way of saying Black people need to be policed more harshly.

Imagine when that's coupled with the force multiplier of the stigma often associated with mental illness.

"There's so much public misperception about violence and mental illness. If the public thinks that, then law enforcement is going to think that," says Jennifer Piel, a University of Washington professor who helped launch the university's Center for Mental Health, Policy, and the Law.

And there lies the heart of the problem, and the reason Black people and those with mental illnesses are overrepresented in police shootings and in the criminal justice system Piel studies. And the reason they are underrepresented in budget considerations.

Bias feeds stigma, and stigma bias.

It's a reason we've continued hacking at our state's mental health budget even before our pandemic without much resistance. Currently, King County's Mental Illness and Drug Dependency program stares down a projected $42 million shortfall.

"[T]here is no replacement for a well-funded mental health system and increased cross-system coordination of services between medical care, mental health services, and the criminal justice system," says Piel.

Budgets, policing, policy are nothing more than visible instruments of our society, crafted with entrenched prejudices, fears, and ignorance.

Until our society commits itself to narratives rivaling our current biases, and not merely responding to those biases' symptoms, we'll continue having ornamental pledges to social change vanish upon backlash.

Imagine narratives not equating Black people with a need for social control or those casting people with mental illnesses as social defects.

For them, life and death would no longer rest on chance, but consideration.

Reparations Can Take Many Forms. Let's Start by Being Honest About What We've Wrought

There is no resolution I crave more than for us to stop binging on lies. Like most opiates, they are as lethal to progress as they are numbing to awareness.

My desire catalyzed nearly four years ago as I moderated a panel discussion of *I Am Not Your Negro* in Columbia City. A multiracial audience packed the Ark Lodge Cinemas to watch the James Baldwin documentary. With narration by Samuel Jackson, the famed writer spoke on the pervasiveness of white power in American society, and its destruction of the humanity not only of Black people, but of all people, including white ones.

Moments after the credits rolled, the theater was filled with a heavy solemnness as people bowed their heads in reflection, some even tearing up.

Here, I thought, is finally a moment where we shed the infantilism inherent in favoring mythology over truth. Here is a moment where we can face what we've been and done as a country, and a city. Here is where we go about the business of reconciling our past accounts with our present-day aspirations.

It took a grand total of 30 minutes for that balloon to deflate.

During the audience Q&A an Alabama transplant gushingly praised Seattle, for how much it wasn't Alabama. To be in a theater with multiple races meant we "were doing things right here."

The majority white audience burst out in applause.

The majority of people of color on the panel exhaled leaden sighs.

Seattle may not have the scars of Birmingham, but its wounds are still ghastly.

Belying our city's reputation is the fact that it was committed to segregation early on.

Our inequities parallel those of our nation. And like the rest of America's they are authored by human hands, not those of nature. As the University of Washington's Segregated Seattle project shows, Seattle locked people of color out of the labor force, medical care and entrepreneurship.

But our city's greatest sin may have been its practice of redlining, which confined people of color into housing tracks such as Seattle's Central District that were deemed less desirable. With ZIP codes an increasingly greater determinant of social mobility than work ethic, the discriminatory practice deprived families of the ability to accumulate generational wealth through homeownership.

A Seattleite who grew up in the redlined district of the city in the '80s has a lower income today than a Seattleite who didn't, according to the Opportunity Atlas, which analyzes social mobility data.

It also contributed to the gulf that's defined America as much as football and Coca-Cola.

Name any measure of social misery—incarceration, poverty, homelessness, school expulsions, COVID-19 deaths—and you will find Black people outdistancing white people.

In 1968, the Kerner Commission, tasked by the Johnson administration with studying the origin of the inner city uprisings of the late '60s, said of the destitution that drove the uprisings, "White institutions created it, white institutions maintain it, and white society condones it."

And there lies its remedy.

Duke economist William Darity Jr., who co-authored *From Here to Equality: Reparations for Black Americans in the Twenty-First Century*, pegs closing the racial wealth gap at $10 trillion to $12 trillion. For context, the United States GDP in 2019 was about $21 trillion.

The colossal sum triggers his reservations about localities calling any remunerative efforts reparations, such as those underway in California. Neither states or cities can afford the tab.

"The federal government allowed these atrocities to take place," said Darity, by phone. "It's the federal government who is ultimately responsible."

Darity is also concerned that local efforts billed as reparations could undercut a national push toward true reparations. People could argue that reparations have already happened.

However, this doesn't absolve states or localities. And some are undertaking a public accounting of their past.

"This is about identifying systemic Black policy solutions and eradicating disparities, which no longer make it a liability to be Black," says Chris Rabb, a Pennsylvania state legislator.

Rabb, a Democrat, has put forth a reparations bill he hopes can be used as a framework for other localities, including Seattle.

The bill would create a compendium of historical laws that are explicitly racist, putting past deeds and inaction up for public scrutiny. In Seattle, that would make Article 34 of Code of Ethics for Realtors, wherein the city permitted racial discrimination in housing, open to examination of how it devastated Black generational wealth.

Most critically, his bill would create an individual board to mandate state money be appropriated to historically Black neighborhoods and institutions most impacted by systemic racism. This allocation would persist as long as racial disparities in the state did.

While I agree with aspects of Darity and Rabb's approaches, given that 80% of Americans stand against cash remuneration for descendants of enslaved Africans, I believe a more politically realizable solution exists in universal programs such as "Medicare for All" and equitable education funding—moves that would disproportionately benefit Black people.

Black people would be the targeted but not exclusive beneficiaries of these policies, as evidenced by affirmative action. Billed as a policy prescription for Black uplift, it simultaneously elevated white women.

Locally, Seattle's mayor and City Council have redirected money toward the Black community as part of recent equity initiatives. But reparations talk has been mostly limited to a state environmental task force saying reparations may be needed to address environmental health disparities.

There are grassroots efforts like those of the Seattle Democratic Socialists of America that are developing a reparations fund for monetary compensation to the Black community. The group hopes the fund can serve as a model for larger-scale efforts in the country over time, according to Kelli Branch, a co-chair of Seattle DSA's Afrosocialist caucus.

I have no idea which reparations approach will or won't work nor what is politically possible, given Americans' lack of agreement around wearing a mask for public health considerations.

I do know there is one form of reparations that is immediate, powerful, transformative and painful: a commitment to blunt, inexhaustible truth recited throughout our schools, offices and legislatures.

Knowing what we were, and how that led us to what we are, is the vehicle for any nation, city, or individual seeking maturity and wholeness. Our growth, driven by overcoming our addiction to a fictional America and Seattle, must never cease. And it must extend to the Native, Japanese, Jewish, LGBTQ and several other communities.

Will that create a more equitable country overnight?

No, but it will make us a more honest one.

FOR LATRELL WILLIAMS

CHILDHOOD OFFICIALLY ENDS the moment you learn your friend was murdered.

Before then, regardless of how many years spent bumbling around on this spinning rock, there still exists a faith in the resiliency of tomorrows.

Your heart still clutches tightly to the adolescent conviction that tomorrow's arrival carries with it hope, and luminous possibilities to vanquish whatever darkness engulfs your today.

But that belief evaporates once you hear the person you roamed high school hallways with, the person who helped an awkward loner endure a terrible high school experience, the person who helped you persist in your seemingly delusional passion for writing, died before his time, killed just a mile from your home.

I found out recently that my high school classmate Latrell Willams was identified as the victim in the fatal shooting that took place Tuesday night near the Lakeridge neighborhood. According to police reports, Latrell died after suffering multiple gunshot wounds. No one yet knows exactly what happened, or why, as the case is still ongoing.

Latrell's fatal shooting was one of three to take place in South King County in a week's span—receiving scant attention from our political leadership.

Speculation coming from local television stations, neighborhood social media groups, and Next Door haven alike, followed the typical script re-enacted whenever a black male is killed in a shooting in the South End. It must be a gang thing, the victim himself was probably a gang-banger, a thug, or a homeless person in a dispute over drugs. The usual monikers are painted on an unknown murdered black man, his life now a blank canvas colored in by an ignorant perception.

Initially, I gave only a passing thought about the shooting, caught up in the frenzy of a news cycle continuously vomiting up one dismal tale after the next.

My shame came from recognizing that I too had originally dismissed—just another sad tragedy, a story that happens to often—because I, like the others had casually reduced the life of who I thought was an unknown person, to a stereotype.

And, while I can't speak to every aspect of his life, I can testify to those I knew. Latrell was anything but stereotypical.

My mind raced back to our high school days. Like me, Latrell was a black South Seattle bred student exported to a predominantly white, affluent school. Unlike me, he had hit the genetic jackpot. As the star running back our senior year, his muscles seemed constantly pregnant, about to give birth to another. Black Hercules, the "L-Train", Latrell looked like the love child of granite and titanium.

Despite his talent for athletics, we aligned because we were still two people who never wholly seemed to fit in, unable to completely give away all of ourselves to an atmosphere that rejected a large chunk of our personas.

Each year I did my best to exhaust every absence I could from a school I dreaded attending each morning. I counted down every minute until the clock hit 2:30pm, bringing the sweet salvation of the dismissal bell, and the reprieve it brought from the shame of being black and poor.

But Latrell made my captivity there bearable. The star running back would sit at the cafeteria table with me, right at the exact moment I began thinking I had been placed in contagion because no one dared come within a 10-foot radius.

Naturally laconic, every word he spoke had purpose. He used them to convince a 120-lb, rail-thin, 5-foot-nothing senior to join the football team in during my final year of high school—as much as I hate to admit it, the best experience of my high school years.

It was how he persuaded me to continue showing up to class after I had been warned that one more absence would result in me automatically failing the year. I had the bright idea to simply stop showing up to school so my parents would be forced, or so I thought, to let me finish out high school at Rainier Beach.

It was how he got me out of trouble all those times I was busy doing every single one of those lurid things teenagers swear up and down to their parents they're not doing, but of course are.

It was how he persuaded me to finally enjoy a little bit of my experience at a high school I spent three and a half years hating with the raw intensity of a thousand white-hot suns.

He rarely smiled, as he seemed to always be navigating his place in the school, and the world, along with his future's course as a football recruit, but still fixed in my mind is the one he laid on our graduating class as he was named the athlete of the year. Though he was looking out at all of us, I kept thinking it was directed at me, saying, in his typical understated way, "We South End boys made it."

Our paths diverged after high school, he went off to play football at Montana State, and I went California Dreaming in Los Angeles.

They converged again though, when I returned to Seattle, giving up one fantasy to pursue another.

I began bumping into him almost every day at the Rainier Beach library.

It was the only office space I could afford in the early days of the *Emerald*. He would be there just as religiously working on scripts for a show he had in mind to produce one day, our friendship was rekindled. We talked about our shared love of storytelling, contrasting our chosen mediums. His love for the visual was matched by mine for the written word.

For that, he had my kinship, but he had my respect for the fight he was undertaking.

He shared with me his long, protracted custody battle over his son that had lasted more than a year. The child had been suffering noticeably in a toxic situation. I remember thinking then, the same thoughts as today: in a world where black men are constantly maligned for being absentee fathers to the detriment of their families, here was a determined Latrell obsessed with reuniting with his 12-year-old son, no matter the cost in money or time.

He would keep me regularly updated on the progress, or lack thereof, and we'd encourage each other to show up every day to chip away at our dreams. We struggled, strived and survived in those early days when our dreams seemed to be unable to escape irrelevance, and failure seems inevitable.

But his words lifted my spirit as they had a decade earlier, telling me whether "sprinting, walking, or crawling—just keep moving forward, Marcus."

Months of Sundays have passed since we saw each other last. Childhood really is gone, and with it a reliance on tomorrow's grace to speak words foolishly delayed.

He never waited to speak the ones I needed to hear. I wish I hadn't reserved my own in thanking him for feeding a scrawny kid belief who previously feasted on a steady diet of doubt. I wish I had capitalized on our shared present to express gratitude for steering a reckless teenager's destiny away from the treacherous hazards along life's turnpike. I wish I would've said, "I love you, Latrell."

But as you once told me, it's never too late to do what needs doing.

To Heal Our Collective Trauma We Must First Face It

AMERICANS ARE TRAUMA-RIDDEN PEOPLE. The sooner we admit this, the sooner we can heal.

Our inherited legacy is threaded together from slaughter, slavery, and brutalization, the humanity of millions of Black, brown, Indigenous, poor, trans, and other people sacrificed for this country's prosperity.

Over the span of a month we have seen white supremacists raid our nation's Capitol trying to rip out the throat of our democracy.

Right now, our country is inhabited by a majority of people who perceive each other as our greatest threat, according to a CBS News/YouGov poll.

We are also neglecting to foster our future generations. Children make up a third of all people living in poverty in this country, according to a report from the Center for American Progress. They also make up a growing number of the food insecure, where in our own state, 1 in 7 children struggles with hunger, according to Feeding America.

Here we are: fearful, broken, anxious, and traumatized.

Can we be anything else when there are many of us still unmoored from reality—seduced by lies, and a fabled racial and gender superiority?

Yet, there are still too few of us willing to see our ugliness for what it is, not a "bug" of our democracy but a feature.

As reprehensible as the actions are of those who stormed the Capitol and of our former president's loyal sycophants who prioritize his approval over truth, it is the thought of inaction that stalks me.

Sitting on a stone bench in Rainier Beach's Kubota Garden after the inauguration of Joe Biden and Kamala Harris, I began recognizing a familiar American cultural reflex: the urgency to move on.

It is the answer to most questions demanding social consideration in our country. What about the Red Summer of 1919 when bloodthirsty white mobs massacred Black communities? We move on.

What about the fact that 92% of women murdered by men are killed by a man they know? We move on.

What about our decades of decreased social mobility in a country promising hard work equaling economic uplift? We move on.

We pretend that our proprietary atrocities are not really us.

And in moving on we do nothing but travel with our trauma.

I speak not solely as an observer but as a child produced by this society.

Our national inability to deal with trauma was transmitted to me, as it is many of us. More than three years ago, I attempted suicide.

My near self-extermination came after a buildup of pain (some self-inflicted, some given, some received) that

I tried to disregard for too long in denial. What about my untreated mental illness?

Culturally conditioned, I moved on. It was better than scrutinizing my pain. Instead, I vaulted from harm to harm without stopping long enough to address any particular one.

I shared much in common with the majority of my country kin, according to Liz Covey, a South Seattle-based trauma therapist.

"Our country is different from others. We are a people who have not reconciled our original sins. I think it's actually really affected our psyches," Covey told me during a Zoom interview. "Psychologically we develop defenses to cope with trauma. That's survival mode."

In the heat of trauma, our coping mechanisms, including denial, often give the false impression of resilience. However, many times we are simply deferring the emotional toll of a situation to a later date, according to Covey, who has studied collective trauma.

"We're attempting to cope. But I think we're in survival mode right now," said Covey. "Survival mode is activated when you're enduring trauma. But the trauma needs to be ceased, or at least minimized. You can't heal while triggered."

You also can't heal when you live in a society that doesn't know how. Covey says that's one reason our culture turns to brute force as a way of dealing with problems.

"It comes from our history where that's how we have resolved conflict. It's how we've governed. You can see the brutality in our prison system and in our schools," she said.

My question is what happens when suffering doesn't cease? What happens when an attempted coup follows the latest police killing of Black people, which follows a pandemic, which follows a swell of previous tragedies?

How do we avoid infecting future generations with 245 years worth of unaddressed trauma? How do we not rupture from the inside?

Covey says a partial solution is policies that alleviate basic needs, like universal health care.

I believe another part is a cultural and personal reckoning with why we continuously practice punishment over healing, hubris over humility, and self-absorption over collective reflection.

Those proclivities result in a President Trump, in a coup at our doorstep, and in people believing their self-worth is tied to another's degradation.

We're doomed to repeat this cycle, unless we begin prioritizing healing in a culture that never has. A mighty task that begins with acknowledging that our pain is prominent, but not all we are.

That's why, after the inauguration, I visited Kubota Garden. For me, that's been a healing space when I'd sunk so low I'd wanted to cease living.

As Linda Kubota Byrd, granddaughter of garden founder Fujitaro Kubota, told me, "It's a place you go to reconnect ... to experience a loving, sacred feeling."

I return to the garden repeatedly to process trauma. There I'm free to be the things our society conditions us not to be—messy, complex, vulnerable, accountable, humbled, contrite—but welcomed anyway.

What if all of us could be this?

More than the sublime garden, Kubota's enduring legacy is that, even in this day, our society remains capable of transmitting love, empathy, compassion, and remembrance that you are more than the hurts that drive you.

It is no small reminder.

No, it is necessary for our survival.

Dreamers Must Not Sleep
(The Wages of Wokeness)

We're less than a month into the new year and I've struggled not to wish it was already over.

Nearly every day hatches a fresh absurdity from our national leadership, new drum-beats for war, and routine attacks against the idea of multicultural democracy. (The fact that neo-Nazis, hoping to ignite a race war, planned for mass violence in Virginia on the same day that honors Martin Luther King, Jr. speaks distressing volumes of where we are, and are not, as a country in the 51 years after his death.)

Additionally, I can only imagine the routine indignities many of you have already suffered personally. Perhaps they are similar to mine when a reader, taking offense to a column I wrote about the unique hardships faced by women and people of color running for political office, anonymously mailed me a four page screed, rambling on about how "racist I was against white men," and that if I "and my 'woke warriors' just shut our damn mouths, racism, sexism, and lgbtq-ism (his words), wouldn't be a problem.

For good measure, he gave suggestions on what I could do with his backside.

No, these first three weeks of the new year are almost making me long for 2019… Well…okay…it's not quite that bad.

But this new year's brutal introduction has also affirmed a valuable lesson: That in this very complex, intricately layered world of human invention, as essential as hope is, it can never be enough in and of itself to change our world.

It's not a dearth of hope (or even love) that necessarily shred the connective fibers, whether inside us, between individuals, or among the larger society, a therapist friend of mine recently told me.

Those bonds perish because of a deficiency of possibilities. Possibility is what fuels the foundation from which hope and love catch fire. Without it, they burn away slowly, like wishes turned to ash.

That diagnosis resounds so profoundly on this weekend of commemoration for the only individual to have a federal holiday named in their honor, at a moment when well-trodden cliches tell of how Dr. King's dream remains unfulfilled.

And while I don't disagree, and while Dr. King deserves all of the reverence due to him, what is too often forgotten by all of the perfunctory speeches and punditry is how limited that dream actually was. And how restricted were its possibilities, in part because social transformation does not spring from a solitary architect.

I realize how preposterous that might sound. After all, the vision King laid out 56 years ago speaks so much of unity. It calls for America to live up to its creed of "all men being created equal … and making justice a reality for all of God's children … and the sons and daughters of former slaves and slave owners sitting down at the table of brother-hood."

But I take instruction from Anna Arnold Hedgeman, a primary organizer of the March on Washington where King's famous speech was given. As a black woman, she succeeded in organizing the majority of white Christian allies who showed up on that day. And yet, like all of the women organizers of the march who'd put in just as much if not more work than their male counterparts, she was denied not only an opportunity to speak, but her rightful place at the front of the line.

Though she respected him, she always thought King's dream was too inadequate for the one desperately needed by society. She would say as much decades later, telling friends, "Martin said I ... I have a dream ... And to this day I wish he hadn't. I wish he had said 'we.' ... 'We have a dream' ... That would have been for all those people who had and continue to presently dream in vain."

I believe, much like Anna did, that it's partially for that reason that, for as much progress as was made during and because of our civil rights movement, it stopped short of ir-revocably transforming our society to the point that it could not indulge an aspiring, authoritarian despot while a sizable minority cheers his cruelty and prejudice.

Because you see, "we" doesn't just invite others to dream, it requires their counsel in constructing that possibility.

"We" doesn't tolerate women performing acts of labor for a movement that denies them voices of influence. "We" doesn't command many of those same women to keep silent about the sexual assault committed against them by members of that same movement.

"We" does not set aside the contributions of members from the LGBTQ community like Bayard Rustin, who was largely responsible for the adoption of non-violence by a plurality of the civil rights movement, including King.

"We" does not table addressing the collective struggles of others simply because individual members from marginalized groups are given "conditional" seats of economic and political power as long as they don't speak too loudly about the trauma visited upon members of their community.

"We," for some of us, means fully accepting that society selectively advantages certain identities (our sex, our race, our gender, our able-bodiedness)—and demands we do not reflexively fall into a defensive stance when faced with critiques of those benefits and the oppressive systems they spawn from. It means when you are asked to identify these social forces at play—whether in your behavior, or your workplace, or your church—you are able to view it as an invitation to collectively devise strategies to overthrow those forces.

"We," for others of us, means forgoing the vanity that comes with making a public spectacle of our "divine social righteousness" to give grace to those who are attempting to unlearn a lifetime of social conditioning. "We" means not rushing to equate a knowledge gap with bigotry, allowing a person errors (but correctives) along the bridge they travel to becoming a better person.

"We" replaces the word "woke" (and its implication of a lifetime degree in social justice enlightenment) with the word "growth" (and its ongoing education in how to accept that we are all spectacularly, frustratingly complex human beings). Inside each of us rages a war between good and evil, kindness and cruelty, courage and fear, doubt and faith, the desire to seek, and the will to find.

Because "we" is not conformity to some undefined notion of unity that too often implies a collective pledge to fall silent over the sins of the status quo.

"We" is a long arduous journey to the formulation of a living, breathing, rendered possibility of "social wholeness"—a wholeness formed from connecting our jagged but congruent parts. That journey requires patience with ourselves and each other, constant learning, a fidelity to empathy, and a commitment to giving and receiving healthy instruction on how "we" build a better world.

It is that possibility that is the hope with teeth—a fierce kind of love that endures the loss of a sole individual. It does so because it is the progeny of so many who fight, strive, and live for a just world. So many who refine, remake, falter, flounder, fall, and fall again so that "we" can rise and rise again in pursuit of that possibility.

And it's that possibility—for what "we" can become as a world, as a city, as a congregation—that fuses us and allows us to embrace larger lives and larger worlds than "I" could have ever dreamed alone. It's that possibility that endures even when hope is punch-drunk.

Because it wasn't hope alone that led our indigenous brothers and sisters to survival when every government policy sought their eradication. It wasn't hope alone that enfranchised the fight for the liberation of enslaved Africans when the Emancipation Proclamation was still generations away. It wasn't hope alone that fueled the women's suffrage movement or marriage equality for all until both were realized.

It was a collectively imagined and drawn possibility of what this world and those in it could one day become.

I ask you now, what will "we" become as human beings sitting next to each other in our offices, in our homes, in our schools, and our city halls, so that our conceived possibility can filter through, up and around our country, our society, and our world, becoming stronger, bigger, and bolder?

There is a folk proverb that I repeat when I find myself overwhelmed by adversity. It goes: "There is a flower so exquisite in its beauty that spending the entirety of your life searching for it, without ever finding it, is not a wasted life."

There is a world whose conception is so beautiful that it is worth a lifetime's work.

May "we" dream of it together.

Naomi Osaka Prioritized Her Mental Health. It's Time We Followed Suit

On the last day of Mental Health Awareness Month, in May, I hooted louder for Naomi Osaka than I ever have for any athlete, and she was nowhere near a tennis court.

Despite being well-positioned to earn her fifth Grand Slam title, Osaka prioritized her mental health and withdrew from the French Open on Monday.

Her decision came after she was fined by tournament organizers and criticized by media personalities for refusing to speak with the press. In her refusal, she had cited her concerns over how those interactions might impact her depression and anxiety.

Many won't view her actions in the same courageous light as former NFL quarterback Colin Kaepernick's taking a knee against police brutality. Osaka hasn't lost her tennis career. But she did elevate a much-needed conversation about mental health in this country.

In 2019, nearly 52 million Americans suffered from mental illnesses but only 44.8% received any type of treatment for them, according to the National Alliance on Mental Illness. Dealing with an untreated mental illness means you're more likely to attempt suicide, develop a substance abuse disorder, or engage with law enforcement.

Per a OnePoll study, 62% of us dread our boss's contempt should we ask for time off to recalibrate our mental health, despite the Family and Medical Leave Act explicitly allowing us to.

I understand why.

Three years ago, fear of jeopardizing my career nearly stopped me from telling my editor at *The Seattle Times* that I needed an extended break. I'd been employed there less than a year.

I broke down in tears in her office. I'd already broken down mentally weeks prior.

I expected her ridicule. She instead offered her support. With her blessing, I temporarily relocated to Fort Worth, Texas, to recoup.

There, I could walk the streets anonymously with no obligation to do anything but heal.

It provided the perfect sanctuary for a mind that became a boomerang of torment. My brain ceaselessly shrieked that I was unlovable, unworthy and grotesque.

The loop of self-devaluation was one of the reasons I contemplated suicide on more than one occasion, including the night I walked out of my editor's office.

Despite all evidence to the contrary, I felt I'd let her and my entire community down. In my mind, all the naysayers who believed a Black man without a traditional journalism background could never cut it at a big-city newspaper had been proven correct. I plummeted into depression.

As I obsessed on death, memories of my Aunt Sheila came into view. Snared by depression, she'd taken her own life when I was 4, leaving a daughter and other grieving loved ones.

That tragedy stays with my family to this day. Not wanting to cause them another one, I became determined to seek help.

Unfortunately, when you're recovering from a mental health crisis there's no typical journey. You're restricted to what you can do, including educating yourself about your condition and finding the right doctor, therapist, and medication.

After that, your recovery is anyone's guess. Perhaps a week will pass, maybe a month, or a year.

All you can do is wait for the poetry to return inside of you, supplanting the stubborn emptiness that's there.

But if you're lucky, all those people you were afraid to tell about your struggles will be there to remind you of the resiliency you've shown in surviving adversity in your life.

They show you that admitting your mental health struggles will never equate to inadequacy.

I wish I could tell you that the years since that Fort Worth trip have stopped my mind from whispering suggestions of suicide, or that my depression never becomes so debilitating that it sometimes takes days to write an article that should take 30 minutes.

What I can tell you is the community of support consisting of friends, family, therapists, and colleagues has made facing those challenges manageable. There are no perfect days but there are better ones.

Honesty is the one thing that publicly acknowledging your mental health struggles will guarantee you.

And our society is literally dying for the truth.

HOME IS A PLACE CALLED KUBOTA GARDEN

As a lifelong Seattleite (a lifelong South Seattleite, actually), I was asked to share what Kubota Garden means to me. Now that's a pretty simple question—with a very hefty answer, given my relationship with the garden that has ranged from when I was a teenager to today.

Throughout that time, Kubota Garden has epitomized the most powerful one-syllable word in the English language.

And no, that word isn't "love" (as powerful as it is). That word is "home." Because home (at least an ideal one) is where human love, peace, fortitude, and belonging are nurtured and absorbed.

Home is a place that goes beyond just welcoming you—it accepts you for all you are, whatever you may be. You need no invitation to enter its safety and its refuge.

Kubota Garden first showed me how powerful the concept of "home" is as a teenager who was trying to do all he could to find himself ... and fit in and search for any identity that was compatible with a school where I was one of the few Black kids and a life outside of school where I had my Blackness constantly challenged by some in my community who believed I thought myself superior to them because of my private education.

At that stage of my life, on any given afternoon, I'd hear myself called "tar baby" and then a few hours later have to turn around and fight kids who lived near my neighborhood on my way back home from school. It all added up to a recipe of alienation—with me never feeling as if I belonged anywhere.

Anger began to have a constant grip on me, and that fury eventually mixed with depression and apathy. My spirit began to metabolize all the toxicity and negativity fed to me daily.

It was around that time I found myself walking up Renton Avenue raging internally at a world that didn't seem to want me.

And like a magnetic force, Kubota Garden drew me to it.

As I entered the garden I passed stone benches, hydrangeas in bloom, koi-filled ponds, and birches—it emanated something I'd rarely had in my life up to that point: Stillness. And grounding.

Kubota soon became my remedy to painful insults and regular fisticuffs. So much so that there were days I'd skip school to stay in the garden all day, storing up enough peace I found in its sanctuary to equip myself for the world outside.

The garden trumpeted this inaudible but somehow still visceral language of serenity that my spirit felt fluent in.

It was a language shared by others in the garden, whom I saw engaged in reflection and meditation.

At the time, Kubota Garden was a part of one of the most diverse zip codes in the United States, but ironically it was one of the few places where I actually witnessed the mingling of my vibrant South Seattle community: Black, white, Asian, Pacific Islander, Japanese, Chinese, Somalian, Jewish, and so many, many more, together, their humanity hugged and affirmed by the boundaries of Kubota Garden. For those brief spells in Kubota, I witnessed an America that proclaims an equality and solidarity of humanity. That America that most of us hope for—but know rarely exists in practice—was here on display for me every day.

Honestly, the time I spent at Kubota is what got me through those days of adolescence when I was on the brink of engaging in self-destruction and self-harm.

Just by its accessibility, Kubota made me feel "gotten" and validated.

Now, I wish I could say that was the last time I ever needed to lean on the garden to help me get through life or process adversity, but in some ways it was just the beginning.

You see, I started developing a pattern in life where I swung between stability on one end and havoc on the other.

And that pattern inevitably left a trail of fractured friendships, broken promises, and a full roster of loved ones I disappointed ... including myself.

I didn't know it at the time, but I had untreated bipolar disorder.

Unaware of my mental illness, I lived often with a volatile mind. In those moments, the only place I could find peace from what felt like an onslaught of carnage was Kubota.

It was there for me at times when few others were. It was there when I couldn't locate love any place else.

It was there as I slowly began to repair and mend my life, after accepting my diagnosis. It was there through every heartache, every amend that I needed to make, every time tragedy threatened to sink me, it was there as a revelation of the splendor of overcoming the inevitable hardships of life.

This garden's founder endured racial discrimination, prison camps, and economic distress to produce and nurture magnificence.

I remember that every time I visit the garden, whether I'm accompanied by joy, pain, sorrow, ardor, wonder, or awe…

The garden calls to me just the same, with an embrace of home.

It's a call resembling the Persian poet and Sufi mystic Rumi's verse (and I'm going to paraphrase ever so slightly):

Come, come, whoever you are. Wanderer, worshipper, lover of leaving. It doesn't matter. Ours is not a garden of despair. Come, even if you have broken your vows a thousand times. Come, yet again, come, come.

And that is why *home* is the most powerful one-syllable word in the English language.

Because HOME is a reminder of life's beauty, endearment, dignity, and worth.

Over these last few years we've spent so much time, too much time, focused on the shadows cast by people who perpetuate hate and fear. We've spent so little time on the sunbeams shone by people who spent their lives nurturing community and transmitting love through their life's work.

But that is what Fujitaro Kubota did with his life, and my life is enhanced because of it. He was an immigrant to this country who created his spectacular garden to feel more at home, and in doing so, he ended up constructing a place where I and so many others always felt the most at home.

AFTERWORD

As I write this, an age of rage and exhaustion blitzes us.
With the daily convergence of catastrophes, I fault no one
willingly surrendering to the onslaught of our circumstances. Nor can I argue with anyone's acceptance of the triumph
of anger, fear, and incompetence over love, compassion, and
reason in our society.

And yet, I know of no time in human history absent
the temptation to submit to whatever bleakness blanketed
the day.

To be overcome by the darkness inherent in our spe-
cies, is as human as our inherent ability to overcome it.

This overcoming is where my focus has shifted over these
last months of uprisings, pandemics, and insurrections.

In this time I have borne witness to those who have
ceased talking about what it means to be a good person, to
go about the hard work of actually becoming one.

I paid witness to those who have somehow defied their
pain, and willingly choose to extend grace, healing, and
justice, to others and themselves.

My own eyes have seen people, who even in the midst of horrendous winters, somehow retain the imagination to dream of majestic springs.

And with it all, I have recognized that true power and liberation come from the elevation of others onto a platform of unprejudiced humanity in a world prone towards unfairness, unjustness, and brutal oppression.

These actions create a world of human flourishing and possibility that must always battle, perhaps without resultation, the world of human disgust and atrocity.

Each of these worlds is within us. Each seeking victory. Each asking for its champions.

One of these is readying to rise, readying to challenge the other.

I hope the words within this book have led you to pick a side.

Marcus Harrison Green
1/13/21

Acknowledgements

The essays in this collection would have never come about if not for the thought, love, and belief given to me by so many. In no particular order, other than beginning with the people who brought be into this world, I'd like to thank:

Phillip Green, Cynthia Green, Latonya Anderson, Antonio Foster, D'Marcus Coleman, Donna Nickelberry, Debra Roper, Gary Roper, Nolan Nickelberry, Sonya Hubbard, Colleen Murphy, Yvette Sampson, Alex Anderson, Keilon Anderson, Devin Chicras, Vladimir Verano, Michael Charles, Crystal Paul, Toshiko Hasegawa, Reagan Jackson, Marcus Harden, Benjamin Hunter, Sonya Green Ayears, Michele Matassa Flores, Bridgette Hempstead, Mason Bryan, Tyrone Beason, Jerry Large, Carolyn Bick, Lola E. Peters, Jessie McKenna, Sharon Maeda, Marti McKenna, Mark Baumgarten, Tamara Power-Drutis, Greg Hanscom, Michael Maine, Sharon Ho Chang, Anne Althauser, Andrew Johnton, Paul Roberts, Beth Kaiman, Sarah Stueiville, Sean Goode, Enrique Cerna, Sakara Remmu, Glenn Nelson, Georgia McDade, Jennifer Zeyl, Ijeoma Oluo, Jini Palmer, Vernal Coleman, Kelsey Hamlin, Gregory Davis, Syd Fredrickson, John Helmiere, Matt Aspin, Mark Newton, Jeff Shaw.

"The March Up the Mountaintop"(Adapted from a speech given January 15th, 2016 at Mt. Zion Baptist Church in Seattle, WA) • "Superman Taught Me Most of What I Know About Life" (Adapted from a speech given July 21st, 2013 at Westside Unitarian Universalist Church in Seattle, WA) • "It Took Me Years to Believe That Black Lives Matter, Let Alone My Own" (Yes! Magazine, October 17th, 2015) • "Filling Your Own Cup" (South Seattle Emerald, December 18th, 2018) • "What We Dread to Address" (South Seattle Emerald, December 1st, 2014) • "Confessions of an Imperfect Ally" (Seattle Weekly January 31st, 2018) • "Why an Atheist Says Amen" (Adapted from a speech given October 21st, 2013 at Westside Unitarian in Seattle, WA) • "Life Before Death" previously unpublished (January 12th, 2014) • "When Your Only Hero Falls" previously unpublished (April 13th, 2014) • "To Young Storytellers of Color" previously unpublished (July 20th, 2018) • "A Ceaseless Cry" (Seattle Times, July 19th, 2016) • "Searching For Identity In the Land of The Free" (Seattle Weekly, November 1st, 2017) • "Black Lives, White Marchers" (Seattle Weekly, December 27th, 2017) • "Patriarchy and Black Lives" (Seattle Weekly, February 18th, 2018) • "Our Divergent Mourning" (Seattle Weekly, March 26th, 2018) • "A Mind of Carnage" previously unpublished (December 12th, 2018) • "Pandemic Recovery and Gentrification" (Crosscut/South Seattle Emerald, April 8th, 2020) • "From Si'ahl To Seattle: Does A Wealthy City Owe Its First Residents Reparations?" (South Seattle Emerald and Bitterroot Magazine, January 17th, 2020) • "A Troubled Childhood Should Not Be a Precursor To a Life of Crime" (Crosscut/South Seattle Emerald, February 12, 2020) • "Our World Needs More Truth, Fewer Saviors" (South Seattle Emerald, June 1, 2020) • "I Glimpsed Hope in a South Seattle Park" (Crosscut/South Seattle Emerald, June 11, 2020) • "How Can We Heal? Braver Angels Test the Notion of Healing Across Political Divides" (Seattle Times/South Seattle Emerald, November 5th, 2020) • "I Fear Everyday Encounters More Than I Do Hate Groups" (Seattle Times/South Seattle Emerald, December 3rd, 2020) • "How I Survived the Collision of Racism and the Stigma of Mental Illness" (Seattle Times/South Seattle Emerald, October 1st, 2020) • "Reparations Can Take Many Forms. Let's Start by Being Honest About What We've Wrought" (Seattle Times/South Seattle Emerald, January 10th, 2021) • "For Latrell Williams" (published in Emerald Reflections 2: A South Seattle Emerald Anthology, 2018) • "To Heal Our Collective Trauma We Must First Face It" (Seattle Times/South Seattle Emerald, February 4th, 2021) • "Dreamers Must Not Sleep (The Wages of Wokeness)" (Adapted from a talk given at Westside Unitarian Church on January 19th, 2020) • "Naomi Osaka Prioritized Her Mental Health. It's Time We Followed Suit" (Seattle Times, June 3rd, 2021) • "Home Is A Place Called Kubota Garden" (South Seattle Emerald, February 20th, 2021)

About the Author

Marcus Harrison Green is the editor-in-chief and co-founder of the *South Seattle Emerald*. He writes a regular column on South Seattle personalities, social movements, juvenile justice and American society, and he is an op-ed columnist for *The Seattle Times*. He is a former scholar-in-residence at Town Hall Seattle, a past Reporting Fellow with *YES!* Magazine, and a recipient of *Crosscut*'s Courage Award for Culture. He is the editor of *Emerald Reflections: A South Seattle Emerald Anthology, Emerald Reflections 2: A South Seattle Emerald Anthology,* and *Fly to the Assemblies: Seattle and the Rise of the Resistance.* He currently resides in Seattle's Rainier Beach neighborhood.

CPSIA information can be obtained
at www.ICGtesting.com
Printed in the USA
FSHW011546070921